Air Fryer Cookbook for Beginners 2021

Delicious, healthy, appealing, and easy to make, Air Fryer Recipe collection for beginners.

AILEEN WILLIAMSON

© Copyright 2021 AILEEN WILLIAMSON All rights reserved.

This document is geared towards providing exact and reliable information in regard to the topic and issue covered. The publication is sold with the idea that the publisher is not required to render accounting, officially permitted, or otherwise, qualified services. If advice is necessary, legal, or professional, a practiced individual in the profession should be ordered.

- From a Declaration of Principles which was accepted and approved equally by a Committee of the American Bar Association and a Committee of Publishers and Associations.

In no way is it legal to reproduce, duplicate, or transmit any part of this document in either electronic means or in printed format. Recording of this publication is strictly prohibited, and any storage of this document is not allowed unless with written permission from the publisher. All rights reserved.

The information provided herein is stated to be truthful and consistent, in that any liability, in terms of inattention or otherwise, by any usage or abuse of any policies, processes, or directions contained within is the solitary and utter responsibility of the recipient reader. Under no circumstances will any legal responsibility or blame be held against the publisher for any reparation, damages, or monetary loss due to the information herein, either directly or indirectly.

Respective authors own all copyrights not held by the publisher.

The information herein is offered for informational purposes solely and is universal as so. The presentation of the information is without contract or any type of guarantee assurance.

The trademarks that are used are without any consent, and the publication of the trademark is without permission or backing by the trademark owner. All trademarks and brands within this book are for clarifying purposes only and are owned by the owners themselves, not affiliated with this document.

Table of Contents

Introduction 8

Chapter 1: Air Fryer Basics 9

What is an Air Fryer? 9

What Can You Cook in An Air fryer? 9

General Tips for Air Frying 10

How to Clean Your Air Fryer 12

Benefits of Air Fryer 14

Chapter 2: Air Fryer Breakfast Recipes 16

Air fryer French Toast Sticks 16

Tex-Mex Air Fryer Hash Browns 17

Air Fryer Churros 19

Sausage Patties 20

Air Fryer Breakfast Frittata 21

Air Fryer Scrambled Eggs 22

Avocado and Egg Pizza Toast 23

Air-Fryer Breakfast Croquettes with Egg & Asparagus 24

Air Fryer Mini Quiches 26

Grilled Cheese Sandwich 27

Bacon and Egg Breakfast Biscuit Bombs 28

Air Fryer Breakfast Casserole 29

Air Fryer Hard-Boiled Eggs 30

Air Fryer Everything Bagels 30

Blueberry Bread 32

Air Fryer Breakfast Flautas 33

Air Fryer Breakfast Potatoes 34

French Toast Cups with Raspberries 35

Chapter 3: Air Fryer Chicken Recipes 37

Air Fryer Chicken Tenders 37

Air Fryer Chicken Fajitas 38

Chicken Drumsticks with BBQ Sauce 39

Air Fryer Lemon Pepper Wings 41
Chicken Nuggets 42
Air Fryer Pineapple Chicken Skewers with Curry Dip 43
Sweet and Sour Chicken 45
Chicken Meatballs 46
Air-Fryer Nashville Hot Chicken 47
Air Fryer Chicken Caprese 49
Pretzel Chicken Cordon Bleu 50
Air Fryer Stuffed Chicken Breast 51
Air Fryer Chicken Parmesan 52
Air Fryer Orange Chicken 53
Chicken Taquitos 55

Chapter 4: Air Fryer Meat Recipes 57

Air Fryer Steak Bites and Mushrooms 57
Roast Beef – with Herb Crust 59
Air Fryer Beef and Bean Chimichangas 60
Beef Steak Kabobs 61
Air Fryer Corned Beef Hash 62
Air Fryer Meatballs 63
Air Fryer Steak Fajitas 64
Beef Chips 65
Air Fryer Meatloaf 66
Crispy Roast Pork Belly 67
Air Fryer Pork Tenderloin 68
Air Fryer Tonkatsu 69
Air-Fryer Ground Beef Wellington 70
Beef Satay 72
Air Fryer Mongolian Beef 73
Lamb Chops 74
Air Fryer Baby Back Ribs 75
Stuffed Peppers 76
Turkey Burgers with Zucchini 77

Low-Carb Air Fryer Scotch Eggs 78

Chapter 5: Air Fryer Fish and Seafood Recipes 80

Zesty Ranch Air Fryer Fish Fillets 80

Air Fryer Catfish with Spicy Tartar Sauce 81

Fried Shrimp 82

Air Fryer Fish Sticks 84

Air Fryer Garlic Butter Salmon 86

Air Fryer Cod with Lemon and Dill 87

Air Fryer Shrimp with Lemon and Pepper 88

Tuna Steaks 89

Fish Nuggets 90

Pesto Walnut Fish Fillets 91

Bacon-Wrapped Shrimp 92

Low Carb Tuna Casserole 92

Air-Fryer Fish Cakes 93

Air-Fryer Scallops with Lemon-Herb Sauce 94

Air Fryer Bang Bang Shrimp 95

Cheesy Egg and Tuna Bake 97

Chapter 6: Air Fryer Vegetable Recipes 98

Air Fryer Roasted Cauliflower 98

Air-Fried Beet Chips 99

Air-Fryer Roasted Green Beans 100

Potato and Kale Nuggets 100

Air-Fryer Acorn Squash Slices 101

Air Fried Eggplant (Gluten-Free) 102

BRUSSELS SPROUTS 103

Vegetable Stuffed Potato Patties 104

Air Fryer Onion Rings 106

Air Fryer Seasoned Asparagus 108

Garlic-Herb Fried Patty Pan Squash 108

Air Fryer Potato Chips 109

Air Fryer Vegetarian Momos 110

Air Fryer Pumpkin Fries *111*
Zucchini Corn Fritters *112*
Air-Fried Radishes *114*
Mexican Air Fryer Corn on the Cob *114*
Air Fryer Patatas Bravas *115*
Air-Fryer Green Tomato Stacks *117*
Air Fryer Carrots *118*

Chapter 7: Air Fryer Snack Recipes **120**
Apple Chips *120*
Air-Fried Mozzarella Sticks *122*
Tater Tots *123*
Chickpea Fritters with Sweet-Spicy Sauce *124*
Air-Fryer Turkey Croquettes *125*
Air Fryer French Fries *126*
Air-Fryer Crispy Chickpeas *127*
Air fryer cheez-it recipe *128*
Pepperoni Pizza Fries *129*
Air Fryer Apple Cinnamon Rolls *130*
Air Fryer Roasted Almonds *131*
Air Fryer Falafels *132*
13. Air-Fryer Ravioli *134*
Nutella Banana Sandwich *135*
Mini Pizza *136*
Air Fryer Plate Nachos *137*
Beef Taco Fried Egg Rolls *138*
Air Fryer Roasted Pineapple *140*
Mac and Cheese Bites *140*
Air Fryer Crab Cakes *141*
Crispy Air-Fried Buffalo Tofu *143*
Air Fryer Corn Dogs *144*
Taco Lasagna *145*
Fried Pork and Bok Choy Dumplings with Dipping Sauce *146*

Air-Fryer Caribbean Wontons *148*

Chapter 8: Air Fryer Dessert Recipes 150
Grilled Peaches *150*
Air Fryer S'mores *151*
Air Fryer Oreos *152*
Air Fryer Apple Crisp *153*
Air Fryer Brownies *154*
Strawberry Cheesecake Chimichangas *155*
Air Fryer Beignets *157*
Monkey Bread *158*
Apple Fritters with Brown Butter Glaze *159*
Air Fryer Lava Cake *161*
Air Fried Banana *162*
Air Fryer Blueberry Pie Egg Rolls *163*
Air Fryer Twix Cheesecake *164*
Air Fryer Banana Muffins *167*
Air Fryer Jelly Donuts *168*

Conclusion 169

Introduction

Every day different kitchen accessories and small appliances come from all over the world. The best and most efficient small appliances, on the other hand, are vulnerable in breaking this cycle. The Air Fryer is an example of a small appliance that has taken the culinary world by storm. The Air Fryer has not only won a spot on the kitchen counters of all chefs, but it is still just as valuable and helpful today as it was when the first fryers hit store shelves in 2010.

It's no secret that almost everybody wants balanced, quick, and delicious meals, seven days a week. On the other hand, the fastest dinner options are usually unhealthy and high in grease and salt. Many consumers struggle to find a balance between delicious, fast, and easy meals.

In 2010, the Philips Electronics Company answered the problem of unhealthy meals by introducing the Air Fryer. This brilliant piece of equipment fixed all of your mealtime challenges. When designing this appliance, Phillips engineers paid close attention to every detail. The Air Fryer has a removable tray in the cooking chamber, making it simple to cook and serve. It also ensures that the clean-up process is simple and quick. A valve on the top of the Air Fryer helps filter the air before allowing it to pass through, keeping odors from spreading in your house. A fan built to regulate the internal temperature often protects you from the fryer's fire.

Ultimately, the decision to buy an air fryer comes down to personal preference. Do you want something with a lot of choice and customization, or do you want something simple that just gets the job done?

Air fryers have become the favorite option for many people, especially those trying to avoid oil, or those who value comfort and are looking for an easy-to-use alternative to cook their meals. With wide-ranging models, sizes, and price ranges available, it is simple to find the right air fryer that suits your budget, lifestyle, and cooking needs. With just some basic understanding of how an air fryer works, you'll be cooking in your air fryer like a pro in no time!

Chapter 1: Air Fryer Basics

What is an Air Fryer?

An air fryer is a compact countertop appliance that cooks food by circulating air around it, using convection heating. It distributes heat equally, cooks a little faster, and places the food in a fryer-style basket. It can be used to bake, grill, fry, or roast food. An air fryer works well to give food a crispy, fried texture without adding a lot of fat. Air fryers are versatile parts of machinery with a variety of features ranging from timers to various trays and racks that make cleaning and customization easier.

What Can You Cook in An Air fryer?

You can make a variety of things with an air fryer, whether it's fried chicken, muffins, French fries, or vegetables. Here's a variety of food groups you can prepare with it:

Frozen Foods

Make fish sticks, frozen fries, and nuggets with ease using your air fryer. Preparing these dishes will take no more than 15 minutes.

Baked Food

You'll have to purchase an optional buy accessory, such as a non-stick baking dish, to prepare baked foods. Then you can prepare bread, muffins, custards, lasagna, and so much more.

Meat Dishes

This includes chicken, fish, seafood, beef, or other fried and grilled forms.

Vegetables

After a long day at work, don't miss your nutritious dinner because you can easily prepare steamed and cooked vegetables like broccoli, zucchini, and carrots with an air fryer.

Roasted Nuts

It's easy to roast walnuts, peanuts, and almonds in the air fryer, with it only taking around 5-10 minutes.

General Tips for Air Frying

- Select a suitable place in your kitchen for your air fryer. Always place your air fryer on a level, heat-resistant countertop with at least five inches of space behind it where the exhaust vent is located.
- Make sure you have the right accessories. You may want to invest in additional accessories for your new favorite appliance once you start air frying. You may even

already own some! The only requirement is that the accessory pan fits within the air fryer basket.

- Purchase a spray bottle for the kitchen. Spraying oil on food is better than brushing or drizzling, and overall, it uses less oil. Invest in a hand-pumped kitchen spray bottle if you want to spray foods directly into the basket. It'll be well worth it!

- Make sure the basket isn't too full. Don't crowd the basket with food if you want the best performance. Over-crowding the basket will prevent foods from browning and crisping evenly and take more time overall.

- To achieve evenly browned food, flip the food halfway through the cooking time.

- Check for readiness by opening the air fryer as much as you like. One of the best things about air fryers is that you can open the drawer many times (within reason) to check on the cooking process.

- Use toothpicks to keep foods in place. The fan from the air fryer will sometimes pick up light foods and blow them around. So, use toothpicks to secure foods (such as the top slice of bread on a sandwich).

- Shake the basket. During the cooking process, shake the basket a couple of times to redistribute the ingredients to brown and crisp more evenly.

- Don't be too generous with the oil. If you're going to use the oil, use only a small amount. Excess oil remains in the drawer under the grate, and it will smoke if it builds up too much.

- Use tongs or a spoon to take out the cooked food from the basket. Excess oil collects under the basket's removable grate, so if you take it out and tip it onto a platter, the oil will spill out along with the grate. This can cause you to get burned, make a mess, and result in greasy food.

- To Preheat or Not to Preheat? An air fryer doesn't require a full half-hour to heat up. It only takes a few minutes to preheat. A light on some air fryer models shows when the appliance is preheated. The manufacturers recommend preheating, but you can skip it entirely if you want. If you start your food in a cold air fryer, it only takes three or four minutes longer to cook—no big deal! Try both methods to see which one produces the best results. Preheating also depends on the food you make.

How to Clean Your Air Fryer

So, you purchased an air fryer? If you've tried it, you already know that these trendy kitchen gadgets help you cook all of your favorite fried foods while consuming less fat and calories. After all, you're already cooking, which means you'll have some grease to clean up afterward. Learn how to clean your air fryer with common household items.

Tips for Cleaning Your Air Fryer

Before you clean your air fryer, learn the do's and don'ts for your air fryer maintenance.

- Never put your air fryer in water. Since the main device is an electrical appliance, this will ruin it.

- To clean food particles and residue from your air fryer, avoid using metal utensils, steel wire brushes, or abrasive sponges. Your air fryer's nonstick coating can be damaged as a result.

- If you notice a foul odor coming from your air fryer, put half a lemon in the basket and leave it for 30 minutes before cleaning it.

How Often Should You Clean Your Air Fryer?

After Each Use

Wash the basket, pan, and tray with warm water and soap each time you use your air fryer or put them in the dishwasher. (Make sure these items are dishwasher safe by consulting the owner's manual.) Also, clean the interior with a damp cloth and a small amount of dish soap. Dry all the parts and reassemble.

After Every Few Uses

Though these steps aren't necessary after every use, doing so on a regular basis will keep your air fryer in good working order. Wipe off the exterior with a damp cloth every once in a while. If there is any residue, let the air fryer cool, then clean it with a damp cloth.

How to Deep Clean an Air Fryer

If it's been a while since you cleaned your air fryer, or you're not sure where to begin, keep reading for step-by-step instructions on how to deep clean an air fryer.

Here's What You'll Need to Clean the Air Fryer:

- Soft-bristle scrub brush
- Dish soap
- Baking Soda
- Damp microfiber cloth, or non-abrasive sponge
- Clean, dry cloth

Instructions

1. Unplug your air fryer. Allow it to cool for around 30 minutes.
2. Take the baskets and pans out of the air fryer and wash with warm soapy water. Leave these parts to soak in hot soapy water for at least 10 minutes before scrubbing with a non-abrasive sponge if any of them have baked-on grease or food.
3. Wipe down the interior with a damp microfiber cloth or a non-abrasive sponge with a bit of dish soap. With a clean, damp cloth, wipe away the soap.
4. Wipe down the heating element with a damp cloth or sponge.
5. Make a paste of baking soda and water to remove any baked-on or hard residue from the main appliance. Use a soft-bristle scrub brush to scrub the paste into the residue, then wipe it away with a clean cloth.
6. Wipe down the exterior with a damp cloth. Using a clean damp cloth, remove the soap.
7. Before reassembling, ensure you dry all removable components and the main unit.

Benefits of Air Fryer

This appliance has a lot of positive features. Here are few advantages of using an air fryer.

Healthier Meals

To get your food crispy and browned in this appliance, you don't need much oil! Most people spritz a little oil on the item before starting the cooking process. The hot air utilizes a small amount of oil, and any excess oil drains away from the food. Nuggets, mozzarella sticks, fresh and frozen fries, onion rings, and chicken wings are all possible with this appliance.

Things cooked in an air fryer cook faster than those cooked in a traditional oven, and the excess oil does not soak into the food. So, it's true that they use less oil and prepare healthier meals!

Using air fryers can promote weight loss.

Fried food consumption is directly linked to an increased risk of obesity. This is due to the calories and high-fat content of deep-fried foods.

Weight loss is promoted by switching from deep-fried, to air-fried foods, and reducing your daily consumption of unhealthy oils'.

Quicker, More Efficient Cooking

Preheat time of air fryers is just a few minutes, and the majority of the heat is maintained inside the appliance. Since this heat is not lost to the surrounding air, food cooks faster than the oven or stovetop. Because the circulating air produces the heat, even frozen foods will cook faster.

Versatility

You can air fry, bake, stir fry, reheat, steam, broil, roast, grill, and even rotisserie in some models. Aside from fries and nuggets, you can make steak, chicken thighs or breasts, stir-fried meats, grilled sandwiches, roasted or steamed vegetables, all kinds of fish, shrimp dishes, and even desserts and cakes. You can also bake a whole chicken or small turkey, as well as a beef or pork roast if your appliance is big enough. They're much more than a frying machine!

Space-Saving

Most units are about the size of a coffee maker. Some models are lightweight and ultra-compact, making them ideal for kitchenettes, dorm rooms, small kitchens, and RVs. In situations where an oven is unavailable, an air fryer may be more efficient than a steamer or toaster oven. If you use it regularly, you'll prefer to keep it on your kitchen counter!

Easy to Use.

The majority of fryers are designed to be extremely simple to use. Just set the time and temperature for cooking, place your food in the basket and wait. Of course, shaking your food once or twice during the cooking process improves the results, particularly for foods like chips, fries, nuggets, and wings. This ensures that the browning is even, and the results are incredible.

Chapter 2: Air Fryer Breakfast Recipes

The air fryer is more than just a healthier way of frying food. It's also your secret weapon for preparing delicious breakfast foods that act as an alarm clock. Here we have recipes that will fulfill all of your morning cravings, whether you want sweet breakfasts like apple fritters, or blueberry bread.

Air fryer French Toast Sticks

Prep Time: 10 minutes

Cook Time: 10 minutes

Servings: 2

Ingredients

- 2 tablespoons of butter or margarine, softened.
- 4 pieces of bread, whatever kind and thickness desired
- 1 pinch of ground cloves
- 2 eggs gently beaten
- 1 pinch of salt
- 1 pinch of cinnamon
- 1 pinch of nutmeg

- 1 teaspoon of icing sugar and maple syrup for garnish and serving.

Instructions

1. Preheat the Air fryer to 180°C.
2. In a bowl, gently beat two eggs, add a few heavy shakes of cinnamon, a sprinkle of salt, and small pinches of ground cloves and nutmeg, and properly mix these ingredients.
3. Butter both sides of the bread and cut them into strips.
4. Dip each strip into the egg mixture and put it in the Air fryer (you will have to cook in two batches).
5. After 2 minutes of cooking, turn off the Air fryer, remove the pan, and spray the bread with cooking spray.
6. Turn the strips over and spray the other side.
7. Return the pan to the fryer and cook for another 4 minutes, checking after a few minutes to ensure that they are frying evenly and not burning.
8. Remove them from the Air fryer when the egg is cooked, and the bread is golden brown.
9. To serve, sprinkle with icing sugar and top with whip cream, or serve with a small syrup bowl for dipping.

Tex-Mex Air Fryer Hash Browns

Prep Time: 15 minutes

Cook Time: 30 minutes

Additional Time: 20 minutes

Servings: 4

Ingredients

- 1 jalapeno, seeded and cut into 1-inch rings
- 1 red bell pepper, seeded and cut into 1-inch pieces

- 1 pinch of salt and ground black pepper, to taste
- ½ teaspoon of ground cumin
- 1 tablespoon of olive oil
- ½ teaspoon of taco seasoning mix
- 1 small onion, cut into 1-inch pieces.
- 1 ½ pounds potatoes, peeled and cut into 1-inch cubes
- ½ teaspoon of olive oil

Instructions

1. Soak the potatoes for 20 minutes in cold water.
2. Preheat the air fryer to 320°F (160 degrees C). Move the potatoes to a large bowl after draining and drying them with a clean towel. Toss the potatoes in 1 tablespoon of olive oil. Place them in an air fryer basket that has been preheated. Set the timer for 18 minutes.
3. In the bowl, put the onion, jalapeno, bell pepper, taco seasoning, 1/2 teaspoon olive oil, ground cumin, pepper, and salt. Toss to evenly mix the ingredients.
4. Remove the potatoes from the air fryer and put them in the bowl with the vegetable mixture. Return the empty basket to the air fryer and set the temperature up to 356°F (180 degrees C).
5. Mix the ingredients of the bowl quickly to evenly combine the potatoes, seasoning, and vegetables. Put the mixture in the basket. Cook for 6 minutes, then shake the basket and cook for another 5 minutes, or until potatoes are crispy and browned. Serve right away.

Notes

- Use fresh potatoes because old ones don't crisp up well and remove the seeds from the peppers. They'll burn up and explode. Add more jalapenos, or use spicier pepper-like habanero or serrano if you want it spicier.

Air Fryer Churros

Prep Time: 10 minutes

Cook Time: 10 minutes

Servings: 8

Ingredients

- 2 tablespoons of granulated sugar
- 1 cup of all-purpose flour
- 1/3 cup of unsalted butter, cut into cubes
- 2 large eggs
- 1 cup of water
- Oil spray
- 1/4 teaspoon of salt
- 1 teaspoon of vanilla extract

For Cinnamon-Sugar Coating

- 3/4 teaspoon of ground cinnamon
- 1/2 cup of granulated sugar

Instructions

1. Set a silicone baking mat on a baking sheet and spray with the oil spray.
2. Add the water, salt, sugar, and butter in a medium saucepan. Over medium-high heat, bring to a boil.
3. Decrease the flame to medium-low and add the flour to the saucepan. Cook, mixing continuously with a rubber spatula, until the dough is smooth and comes together.
4. Remove the dough from the heat and put it in a bowl. Set it aside for 4 minutes to let it cool.

5. Add the vanilla extract and eggs in the bowl and mix it with a stand mixer or electric hand mixer until the dough comes together. The finished product will resemble gluey mashed potatoes. Press the lumps together into a ball with your hands, then move it to a large piping bag with a large star-shaped tip.

6. Pipe churros into 4-inch lengths onto a greased baking mat and cut the ends with scissors.

7. Refrigerate the piped churros for one hour on the baking sheet.

8. Gently move churros to the Air Fryer basket with a cookie spatula; leave some space between churros. Spray the churros with oil spray. You will have to fry them in batches depending on the capacity of your Air Fryer.

9. Air fry for 10 to 12 minutes at 375°F until golden brown.

10. Mix cinnamon and granulated sugar in a shallow bowl.

11. Toss baked churros in the sugar mixture right away. Make it in batches. Serve warm with chocolate dipping sauce or Nutella.

Sausage Patties

Prep Time: 6 minutes

Cook Time: 6 minutes

Servings: 4

Ingredients

- 8 raw sausage breakfast patties

Instructions

1. Preheat the air fryer to 370° F.

2. Arrange the raw sausage patties in a single layer in the air fryer; making sure to leave some space between patties.

3. Cook for 6 to 8 minutes, or until the internal temperature reaches 160° F.

4. Take out from the air fryer and serve right away.

Notes

- This time duration is for small breakfast patties. If your patties are much larger, you may have to cook them for a longer duration.

How to Cook Frozen Sausage Patties?

1. Preheat the air fryer to 400° F.
2. In the air fryer, arrange the frozen sausage patties and cook for 4 to 5 minutes, or until thoroughly cooked.

How you can reheat sausage patties in the air fryer:

1. Preheat the air fryer to 350° F.
2. Warm the sausage patties in the air fryer for 3 to 5 minutes, and serve.

Air Fryer Breakfast Frittata

Prep Time: 15 minutes

Cook Time: 20 minutes

Servings: 2

Ingredients

- 3 tablespoons of heavy cream double cream
- 1 green onion sliced
- 4 tablespoons of grated cheddar cheese
- 4 tablespoons of chopped spinach
- 2 tablespoons of fresh chopped herbs of choice
- 4 mushrooms sliced
- Salt to taste
- 4 eggs
- 3 grape cherry tomatoes, halved

Instructions

1. Preheat the air fryer to 350° F/180° C.
2. Line a deep baking pan with parchment paper, then oil it and set it aside.
3. Whisk the eggs and cream together in a bowl.
4. Put the remaining ingredients into the bowl and mix to combine.
5. Put the mixture into the baking pan and place it in the air fryer basket.
6. Cook for about 12 to 16 minutes, or until the eggs are cooked through. Insert a toothpick into the middle of the Air Fryer frittata to see if it's completely cooked. If it comes out clean, then the eggs are cooked.

Notes

- Because the eggs can stick to the pan, it's important to line it with parchment paper and then oil it.
- If you don't want your breakfast frittata to be too brown on top, cover it with foil before cooking and remove it halfway through.
- Feel free to add the vegetables in this recipe that suit your taste. Just make sure to stick with quick-cooking vegetables. This breakfast frittata is an excellent way to use any leftover meat. Add shredded chicken, crumbled bacon, or diced ham if desired.

Air Fryer Scrambled Eggs

Prep Time: 3 minutes

Cook Time: 9 minutes

Servings: 2

Ingredients

- 2 eggs
- 1/8 cup of cheddar cheese
- 1/3 tablespoon of unsalted butter

- Salt and pepper to taste
- 2 tablespoons of milk

Instructions

1. Melt the butter in an oven or air fryer-safe pan in the air fryer.
2. Cook for about 2 minutes at 300°F, or until the butter has melted.
3. Add the milk, eggs, pepper, and salt to a bowl and mix these ingredients.
4. Place eggs in the pan and cook at 300°F for 3 minutes, then stir them around by pushing them to the inside of the pan.
5. Cook for 2 more minutes, then add in the cheddar cheese and mix it.
6. Cook for further 2 minutes.
7. Take them out of the air fryer and serve right away.

Avocado and Egg Pizza Toast

Prep Time: 15 minutes

Cook Time: 10 minutes

Servings: 4

Ingredients

- 3 eggs
- 1/4 cup of shredded Mozzarella cheese
- 1 avocado thinly sliced
- 1/2 cup of shredded cheddar cheese
- 4 pieces of bread, sides trimmed
- Salt and pepper to taste
- 1/4 cup of mayonnaise divided

Instructions

1. Preheat the air fryer for about 2 minutes at 400° F (200° C).
2. Gently grease a springform pan (about 6 inches). Arrange the bread in a sequence so that they fully cover the bottom of the pan. Use your fingers to press down the overlapping areas.
3. Spread 3/4 cup of mayonnaise on the bread, then top with 3/4 cup of the cheddar cheese. Place the avocado slices along the pan's walls and inside so that it looks like a peace sign. Three sections for the eggs are produced as a result of this.
4. Crack 1 egg into each section and add the remaining mayonnaise into each egg. Season the eggs with pepper and salt.
5. Top the avocado slices with the remaining cheese. When the cheese is placed on top of the avocado, it prevents the avocado from being bitter after air frying.
6. Place the pan in the air fryer for about 6 to 8 minutes at 350°F (175°C).
7. Then, top with Mozzarella cheese and air fry for another 2 to 3 minutes at 350°F (175°C), making sure the egg whites are fully cooked through.

Air-Fryer Breakfast Croquettes with Egg & Asparagus

Prep Time: 30 minutes

Cook Time: 20 minutes

Servings: 6

Ingredients

- 6 large eggs hard-boiled, chopped
- 3 tablespoons of all-purpose flour
- 1/2 cup of chopped fresh asparagus
- 1-3/4 cups of panko breadcrumbs
- 1/3 cup of shredded cheddar cheese
- Cooking spray

- 3 large eggs, beaten.
- 1 tablespoon of minced fresh tarragon
- 3/4 cup of 2% milk
- 1/4 teaspoon of salt
- 1/2 cup of chopped green onions
- 3 tablespoons of butter
- 1/4 teaspoon of pepper

Instructions

1. Melt the butter in a large saucepan over moderate heat. Add flour and stir it for about 1 to 2 minutes, until it is lightly browned and smooth. Gradually whisk in the milk, then cook and stir until the mixture has thickened. Stir in the asparagus, green onions, hard-boiled eggs, cheese, tarragon, pepper, and salt. Refrigerate for at least 2 hours.

2. Preheat the air fryer to 350° F. Make twelve 3-inch-long ovals with 1/4 cup of the egg mixture. Put the eggs and breadcrumbs in different shallow bowls. To coat the logs, roll them in the crumbs, then dip them in egg and roll them in crumbs again, patting to make the covering stick.

3. Arrange croquettes in a single layer on a greased tray in the air-fryer basket in batches, spray with cooking spray. Cook for 8 to 10 minutes, or until golden brown. Turn and spray with cooking spray. Cook for another 3 to 5 minutes, or until golden brown.

Air Fryer Mini Quiches

Prep Time: 10 minutes

Cook Time: 10 minutes

Servings: 4

Ingredients

- 2 large eggs
- 1/2 scallion, sliced
- 12 frozen mini phyllo cups
- 2 tablespoons of heavy cream
- Cooking spray
- 1/2 of a 3-ounce link fully cooked, diced chorizo
- 1/4 cup of shredded pepper jack cheese
- Kosher salt and freshly ground pepper

Instructions

1. Preheat the air fryer to 325° F. Set the foil in the air fryer basket and grease with cooking spray. Arrange the phyllo cups in an even layer in the basket. Fill the cups halfway with scallion, chorizo, and cheese.

2. Add the heavy cream, eggs, and 1/2 teaspoon pepper and salt in a bowl, mix these ingredients, then pour it into the phyllo cups. Cook for 5 to 7 minutes, or until the eggs are puffy.

Grilled Cheese Sandwich

Prep Time: 5 minutes

Cook Time: 8 minutes

Servings: 1

Ingredients

- 2 slices of cheddar cheese
- 2 slices of good regular sandwich bread, or crusty bread
- 1 tablespoon of room temperature butter

Instructions

1. Take two slices of your favorite cheese and two pieces of regular or crusty bread.
2. Place the cheese between the two slices of bread. Apply butter or spray on 1 side of the bread with cooking spray (or butter). Place the butter side down on the air fryer basket and then butter the other side.
3. Preheat your air fryer to 350°F and set the timer for 5 minutes.
4. When the 5 minutes are done, turn the grilled cheese sandwich over so the other side gets toasty and golden brown. Cook for another 3 minutes in the air fryer. Not all air fryers cook the same. If your bread did not brown, you need to cook it for a few minutes longer on each side.

Tip

Because of the circulating air at the top of the air fryer, the bread may sometimes move when frying. You can use the trivet that comes with most air fryers to put on the bread.

Bacon and Egg Breakfast Biscuit Bombs

Prep Time: 35 minutes

Cook Time: 15 minutes

Servings: 8

Ingredients

For Biscuit Bombs

- 1 can (about 10.2 oz) Pillsbury Grands! Southern Homestyle refrigerated Buttermilk biscuits (five biscuits)
- 1 tablespoon of butter
- 2 eggs, beaten
- 1/4 teaspoon of pepper
- 4 slices bacon, cut into 1/2-inch pieces.
- 2 oz sharp cheddar cheese, cut into ten 3/4-inch cubes.

For Egg Wash

- 1 tablespoon of water
- 1 egg

Instructions

1. Cut the cooking parchment paper into two 8-inch rounds. Set one round of parchment paper in the bottom of the air fryer basket. Spray with cooking spray.

2. Cook bacon in a non-stick skillet over medium-high heat until it is crispy. Remove bacon from the skillet and put on a paper towel. Gently wipe the skillet with a paper towel. Melt the butter in a skillet over medium heat. Add the pepper and two beaten eggs to skillet; cook, constantly stirring, until eggs are thickened but still moist. Remove from the heat and add the bacon. Give it five minutes to cool down.

3. Each biscuit should be divided into two layers. Make a 4-inch round out of each. Fill each round with one heaping tablespoon of the egg mixture. Add one piece

of cheese on top of each round. Fold the edges up and over the filling, pinching to seal. In a small cup, whisk together the remaining egg and water. Brush the biscuits with egg wash on all sides.

4. In the air fryer basket, place five biscuit bombs, seam side down, on parchment paper. Use cooking spray on both sides of the second parchment round. Place the second parchment round on top of the biscuit bombs in the basket, then top with the remaining five biscuit bombs.

5. Set the air fryer to 325°F and cook for 8 minutes. Remove the top parchment round; gently turn the biscuits with tongs and place in a single layer in the basket. Cook for another 4 to 6 minutes, or until the chicken is fully cooked (at least 165°F).

Air Fryer Breakfast Casserole

Prep Time: 10 minutes

Cook Time: 20 minutes

Servings: 6

Ingredients

- 2 tablespoons of heavy cream
- 1/2 cup of shredded cheddar cheese
- 1 cup of diced tomatoes & green chilies
- 4 eggs
- 2 teaspoons of Italian seasoning
- 1-pound of cooked Italian sausage

Instructions

1. Mix the diced tomatoes, cooked Italian sausage, and Italian seasoning in a large bowl. Mix thoroughly.
2. Sprinkle the melted cheese on top.
3. Add the heavy cream and eggs. Mix it properly.

4. Pour the egg mixture into the ramekins and top with additional shredded cheese.

5. Cook for 5 to 8 minutes at 340°F in your air fryer. Because every air fryer setting is different, make sure the eggs are fully cooked before taking them out.

Air Fryer Hard-Boiled Eggs

Prep Time: 5 minutes

Cook Time: 15 minutes

Servings: 4

Ingredients

- Four eggs
- Salt and pepper to taste

Instructions

1. Preheat the air fryer to 270°F.
2. Cook eggs in the air fryer for about 15 to 17 minutes, preferably on a wire rack.
3. Put the eggs in a bowl of cold water for at least 5 minutes to cool.
4. Peel the eggs and season with pepper and salt, or store in the refrigerator for up to a week.

Air Fryer Everything Bagels

Prep Time: 15 minutes

Cook Time: 30 minutes

Servings: 4 bagels

Ingredients

- 2-1/4 teaspoon of baking powder
- 1 egg, beaten.
- 2 tablespoons of water

- 1 cup of plain non-fat Greek yogurt
- 2 tablespoons of unsalted shelled sunflower seeds
- 1 cup of unbleached all-purpose flour, plus more for dusting work surface
- 1/2 teaspoon of kosher salt
- 1/2 teaspoon of onion powder
- 1/4 teaspoon of garlic powder

For homemade everything seasoning

- 1-1/2 tablespoons of dried minced onion
- 2 tablespoons of dried minced garlic
- 1-1/2 tablespoons of black sesame seeds
- 2-1/2 tablespoons of poppy seeds
- 1-1/2 tablespoons of sesame seeds

Instructions

1. Combine the flour, onion powder, baking powder, garlic powder, and salt in a large bowl. Stir to combine.
2. Add the sunflower seeds and mix.
3. Mix in the Greek yogurt with a rubber spatula until it is well combined. Shape the dough into a ball and place it on a floured surface.
4. Separate the dough into four equal parts. Roll each part in a little flour before rolling into a 10-inch rope.
5. Set a sheet of parchment onto a plate or rimmed baking sheet. Sprinkle a little of the everything seasoning on top.
6. Gently press each bagel into the seasoning. Reshape the bagel if required.
7. Beat an egg with two tablespoons of water. Brush the tops and sides of the bagel with the egg wash before sprinkling with more everything seasoning.

8. Preheat your air fryer to 300° F. You may need to work in batches depending on the size of the bagel. Air fry the bagels for about 12 to 15 minutes, or until golden.
9. Take out from the fryer once done and set aside to cool slightly before slicing and toasting.

For homemade everything seasoning

1. Combine the sesame seeds, poppy seeds, minced garlic, onion, and poppy seeds in a small container.
2. You can store it for 6-12 months.

Blueberry Bread

Prep Time: 5 minutes

Cook Time: 30 minutes

Servings: 5

Ingredients

- 1 ½ cups of frozen blueberries
- 3 cups of Bisquick
- ¼ cup of protein powder
- 3 eggs
- 1 cup of milk

Instructions

1. Combine all ingredients in a bowl and stir until well combined. It will be a thick mixture.
2. Place in a loaf pan and air fry for 30 minutes at 350° F.
3. Insert a toothpick into the bread and see if it's done; if it's done, it will come out clean.

Notes

- On the outside, the bread will be crunchy, while on the inside, it will be soft.

Air Fryer Breakfast Flautas

Prep Time: 15 minutes

Cook Time: 25 minutes

Servings: 4

Ingredients

- 8 eggs, beaten
- 8 fajita size tortillas
- 8 slices cooked bacon
- ½ cup shredded Mexican cheese
- 4 oz cream cheese, softened
- ½ cup cotija cheese (or crumbled feta)
- ½ teaspoon of salt
- ¼ teaspoon of pepper
- 1 ½ teaspoon of cumin
- 1 teaspoon of chili powder
- 1 tablespoon of butter

For Avocado Creme

- ½ cup sour cream
- 1 lime, juiced
- 2 small avocados
- ¼ teaspoon of pepper
- ½ teaspoon of salt

Instructions

1. Melt the butter in a skillet over medium heat. Add eggs and scramble for 3 to 4 minutes until just cooked. Season with chili powder, pepper, salt, and cumin, and remove from heat.
2. In the middle of each tortilla, spread cream cheese. Put one piece of bacon on top of the cream cheese and add scrambled eggs and shredded cheese.
3. Roll tortillas tightly.
4. Place tortillas in a baking dish and brush with melted butter.
5. Press the bake button on the air fryer and set the temperature to 400°F. Cook for 10 to 12 minutes, or until the tortillas are crispy.
6. Remove the tortillas from the air fryer and repeat with the remaining tortillas.
7. In a blender, combine all the avocado creme ingredients and blend at low-medium speed until smooth.
8. Drizzle avocado crème over the flautas and sprinkle cotija cheese on top.

Air Fryer Breakfast Potatoes

Prep Time: 10 minutes

Cook Time: 30 minutes

Servings: 2

Ingredients

- 2 tablespoons of olive oil
- 3 tablespoons of garlic powder
- 3 russet potatoes, chopped into cubes
- ½ teaspoon of black pepper
- 1 teaspoon of chili powder
- 1 teaspoon of sea salt

- 2 tablespoons of paprika

Instructions

1. Wash and chop the potatoes. Drizzle olive oil over the cubes in a large bowl, then add garlic powder, chili powder, and paprika; thoroughly mix all these ingredients.

2. In an air fryer basket, arrange the potatoes in a single layer. Cook for 20 to 30 minutes at 400° F, stirring every 10 minutes so that it cooks evenly. Serve with sriracha ketchup and poached eggs.

French Toast Cups with Raspberries

Prep Time: 20 minutes

Cook Time: 20 minutes

Servings: 2

Ingredients

- 2 oz. of Cream cheese, slice into 1/2-inch cubes
- 1/2 cup of whole milk
- 1 tablespoon of maple syrup
- 1/2 cup of fresh/frozen raspberries
- 2 large eggs
- 2 slices of Italian bread, slice into 1/2-inch cubes

For Raspberry Syrup

- 2 teaspoons of cornstarch
- 1/3 cup of water
- 1 tablespoon of maple syrup
- Ground cinnamon, optional
- 2 cups of fresh or frozen raspberries, divided
- 1/2 teaspoon of grated lemon zest

- 1 tablespoon of lemon juice

Instructions

1. Divide half of the bread cubes into two 8-ounce custard cups that have been greased. Add the cream cheese and raspberries. Top with the remaining bread. Whisk together the milk, eggs, and syrup in a small bowl; pour over the bread. Refrigerate for at least one hour.

2. Preheat the air fryer to 325° F. In an air-fryer basket, arrange the custard cups. Cook for 12 to 15 minutes, or until the custard cups are golden brown and puffed.

3. Meanwhile, whisk together water and cornstarch in a small saucepan until smooth. Add the lemon juice, syrup, 1-1/2 cup raspberries, and lemon zest. Bring to a boil, then reduce the heat. Cook and mix for 2 minutes, or until the mixture has thickened. Strain and remove seeds, set aside to cool.

4. Gently add the remaining half cup of berries into the syrup. Serve with maple syrup and sprinkle cinnamon on top of the French toast cups if desired.

Chapter 3: Air Fryer Chicken Recipes

You can cook everything from chicken wings, breaded chicken, chicken nuggets, chicken meatballs, and fried chicken in an air fryer. It's honestly amazing how many kinds of chicken you can make in this thing.

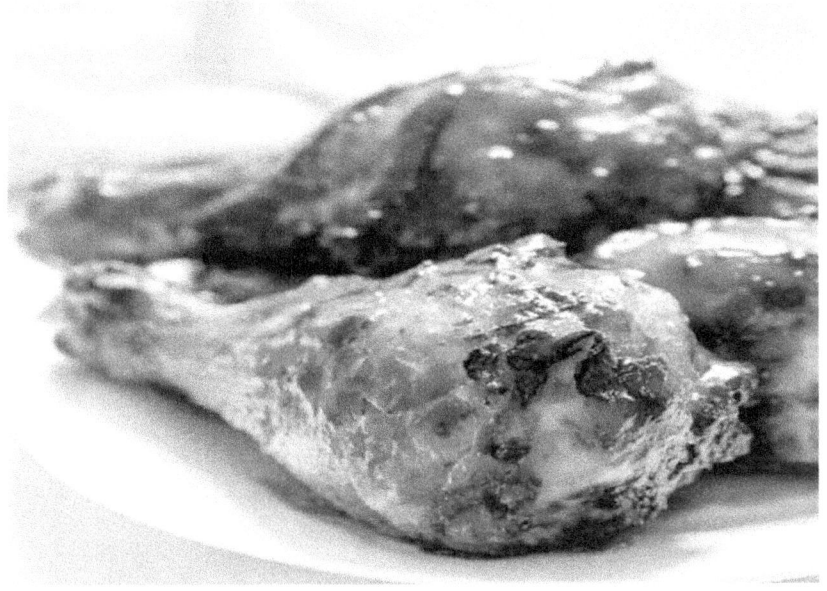

Air Fryer Chicken Tenders

Prep Time: 5 minutes

Cook Time: 30 minutes

Servings: 4

Ingredients

- 2 large eggs, beaten
- 1/2 cup of seasoned breadcrumbs
- 12 chicken tenders (about 1 1/4 lbs.)
- 1 teaspoon of kosher salt
- 1/2 cup of seasoned panko
- Olive oil spray
- Lemon wedges for serving

- Black pepper, to taste

Instructions

1. Sprinkle pepper and salt over the chicken.
2. Break an egg in a shallow bowl. Mix the panko and breadcrumbs in a second shallow bowl.
3. Dip chicken in the egg bowl, then in the breadcrumb mixture, shake off excess, and put on cutting board or in a large dish. Use oil spray on all sides of the chicken.
4. Preheat the air fryer to 400° F.
5. Cook the chicken in batches for 5 to 6 minutes on each side, or until the chicken is well cooked and golden on the outside, and crispy. Serve immediately with lemon wedges.

Air Fryer Chicken Fajitas

Prep Time: 20 minutes

Cook Time: 15 minutes

Servings: 4

Ingredients

- 3 tablespoons of vegetable oil
- ½ onion, sliced
- 1 green bell pepper
- ½ teaspoon of onion powder
- ¼ teaspoon of cayenne pepper
- 1 lb. boneless, skinless chicken breast
- 1 teaspoon of cumin
- ½ teaspoon of paprika
- 1 red bell pepper

- 1 teaspoon of salt
- 1 tablespoon of chili powder
- ¼ teaspoon of sugar
- ½ teaspoon of garlic powder

Instructions

1. Slice the chicken breast into 1/4-inch-thick slices. Slice onion and peppers. Place it in a large bowl.
2. Add the cumin, garlic powder, chili powder, cayenne, onion powder, salt, and sugar in a small dish, and mix it.
3. Add chicken and vegetables in a bowl with three tablespoons of vegetable oil and toss to coat. Add the seasoning mixture and mix it until all ingredients are well coated.
4. Preheat the air fryer to 380° F for 5 minutes. Put all ingredients in the tray or air fryer basket and air fry for 15 to 18 minutes at 380°F. To ensure that everything cooks uniformly, mix everything every few minutes.
5. Serve with warm tortillas or as a salad.

Chicken Drumsticks with BBQ Sauce

Prep Time: 10 minutes

Cook Time: 25 minutes

Servings: 5

Ingredients

- 1/8 cup of extra virgin olive oil
- 1/4 teaspoon of paprika
- 5-6 chicken drumsticks
- 1/4 teaspoon of salt

- 1/2 teaspoon of garlic powder
- 1/2 cup of BBQ sauce (In this recipe Sweet Baby Ray's sauce is used)
- 1/8 teaspoon of pepper
- 1/4 teaspoon of onion powder

Optional

- Pinch of cayenne pepper to add spice.

Instructions

1. Preheat the air fryer to 400° F.
2. Dry the chicken drumsticks with a paper towel.
3. Mix the garlic powder, paprika, olive oil, onion powder, pepper, salt, and cayenne pepper in a bowl.
4. Coat the chicken drumsticks in the oil mixture and massage it for a few minutes.
5. Place the chicken drumsticks in a single layer in the air fryer and cook for 15 minutes.
6. Cook for another 5 minutes after flipping the chicken.
7. Brush all sides of the chicken with BBQ sauce.
8. Cook for 3 to 5 minutes, or until the chicken reaches an internal temperature of 165°F.
9. Remove the chicken from the air fryer, baste more BBQ sauce if desired, and serve.

Air Fryer Lemon Pepper Wings

Prep Time: 5 minutes

Cook Time: 25 minutes

Servings: 4

Ingredients

- 2 teaspoons of McCormick lemon pepper seasoning
- 1 1/2 pounds of chicken wings, drumettes, tips discarded, and flats separated
- 1/4 teaspoon of cayenne pepper

For Lemon Pepper Sauce

- 1 teaspoon of McCormick lemon pepper seasoning
- 3 tablespoons of butter
- 1 teaspoon honey

Instructions

1. Preheat the air fryer to 380° F.
2. Coat the chicken wings with cayenne pepper and lemon pepper seasoning.
3. Put lemon pepper wings in the air fryer basket, don't overload the air fryer basket. Cook for 20 to 22 minutes, shake the basket of wings halfway through cooking.
4. Increase the temperature to 400° F and cook the chicken wings for a further 3 to 5 minutes to get crispy skin.
5. Add the melted butter, honey, and additional lemon pepper seasoning in a bowl and mix it.
6. Take out the chicken wings from the air fryer and drizzle the lemon honey sauce on top. Serve right away.

Notes

How to cook frozen chicken wings in the air fryer?

1. Preheat the air fryer to 380° F.
2. Cook the frozen chicken wings for about 25 minutes in an air fryer. Cook for an additional 5 minutes after increasing the temperature to 400° F.
3. Take the chicken wings out of the air fryer, drizzle the lemon honey sauce, and serve.

How to reheat chicken wings in the air fryer?

1. Preheat the oven to 350° F.
2. Put the chicken wings in your air fryer and cook for 2 to 3 minutes until warmed.
3. Take the wings out of the air fryer and serve right away.

Chicken Nuggets

Prep Time: 15 minutes

Cook Time: 10 minutes

Servings: 4

Ingredients

- 1-pound boneless, skinless chicken breasts, cut into 1-inch cubes
- 1/4 cup of whole wheat flour
- 2/3 cup of whole wheat panko breadcrumbs
- 1/3 cup of grated Parmesan cheese
- 1/4 teaspoon of salt, or to taste
- 1 large egg
- Olive oil spray
- 1/4 teaspoon of black pepper

- Optional dipping sauces: pizza or marinara sauce, ranch dressing, or barbecue sauce
- 2 teaspoons of dried parsley flakes

Instructions

1. Preheat the air fryer to 400° F for 8 to 10 minutes.
2. Place three small shallow bowls on the table. Put the salt, pepper, and flour in the first bowl and whisk lightly. In the second bowl, gently beat the egg.
3. Put the parmesan cheese, parsley flakes, and panko in the third bowl and mix it.
4. Coat the chicken pieces in the flour mixture one at a time, then dip into the beaten egg, then coat into the panko mixture; press gently to stick the coating.
5. Place chicken nuggets in a single layer in the air fryer basket. Don't overcrowd the basket. Use olive oil spray to spray the nuggets (this helps them get crispy and golden brown). Cook each batch of chicken nuggets for 7 minutes, or until the internal temperature reaches 165°F. Don't overcook the chicken nuggets.

Air Fryer Pineapple Chicken Skewers with Curry Dip

Prep Time: 15 minutes

Cook Time: 12 minutes

Marinade Time: 15 minutes

Servings: 4

Ingredients

- 2 small bell peppers (green, red, yellow), cored and cut into 2-inch cubes
- 1 pound of chicken breast, cut into 2-inch cubes
- 1/4 teaspoon of pepper
- 1/2 teaspoon of garlic powder
- 1 teaspoon of salt

- 1/2 teaspoon of onion powder

For the Curry Dip

- 2 tablespoons of mayonnaise
- 1/2 teaspoon of curry powder
- 1 teaspoon of white vinegar or pineapple juice
- 1/2 cup of Greek yogurt
- Salt to taste
- 1 teaspoon of apricot preserves

Instructions

1. In a bowl, season the chicken with garlic powder, pepper, salt, and onion powder. Cover and refrigerate for at least 30 minutes, or up to overnight.
2. Thread chicken pieces on the skewers, alternating between pineapple and bell peppers.
3. In the air fryer basket, set the chicken skewers in a single layer. Gently brush with vegetable or olive oil.
4. Air fry for about 12 minutes at 370° F, or until the thermometer inserted in the thickest part reads 165° F.
5. To make the Curry Dip, whisk together curry powder, apricot preserves, mayonnaise, vinegar, yogurt, pepper, and salt to taste in a bowl. Stir until the mixture is well blended and smooth.
6. Remove pineapple chicken skewers from the air fryer and serve with the curry dip.

Sweet and Sour Chicken

Prep Time: 5 minutes

Cook Time: 10 minutes

Servings: 2

Ingredients

For the Chicken

- 2 tablespoons of cornstarch (or potato starch)
- 1 pound of chicken breasts or chicken thighs, cut into 1 1/2 to 2-inch chunks

For the Sweet and Sour Sauce

- 1/2 cup of brown sugar
- 2 tablespoons of water
- 1/4 teaspoon of ground ginger (or 1 teaspoon freshly grated ginger)
- 3 tablespoons of rice wine vinegar
- 1 tablespoon of soy sauce
- 2 tablespoons of cornstarch
- 1 cup of pineapple juice

Optional

- 1/4 cup of pineapple chunks
- 3-4 drops of red food coloring (for traditional orange look)

Instructions

1. Preheat the air fryer to 400° F.
2. In a bowl, combine the cornstarch and chicken pieces; mix until the chicken is fully coated.
3. Put chicken in the air fryer and cook for 7 to 9 minutes, shaking the basket halfway through. When the chicken is fully cooked, then take it out from the air fryer.

4. Meanwhile, add rice wine vinegar, brown sugar, ginger, pineapple juice, and soy sauce in a saucepan and bring to a simmer for 5 minutes, stirring occasionally.

5. In a separate bowl, make "slurry" with water and cornstarch, then add it to the sweet and sour sauce with the red food coloring and pineapple chunks (if using).

6. Let it simmer for 1 more minute, then remove the saucepan from the heat.

7. Toss the chicken and sauce together, serve with vegetables or rice for a complete meal.

Chicken Meatballs

Prep Time: 10 minutes

Cook Time: 20 minutes

Servings: 4

Ingredients

- 1 lb. of ground chicken
- 1 tablespoon of garlic powder
- 1 large zucchini
- 1 egg, beaten
- Pepper and salt, to taste
- 2 tablespoons of chopped fresh parsley
- 1/2 tablespoon of dried oregano
- 1/2 tablespoon of red pepper flakes

Instructions

1. Preheat the air fryer to 400° F.
2. Use a mesh strainer to finely grate the zucchini. Extract excess water from grated zucchini by adding 1/2 tablespoon salt and set aside. Gently press down the grated zucchini with your fingers to drain excess liquid.

3. In a large bowl, mix the garlic powder, drained zucchini, ground chicken, oregano, red pepper flakes, egg, parsley, pepper, and salt to taste.

4. Using a 1 tablespoon cookie scoop, make sixteen 1-inch balls out of the chicken mixture.

5. Cook the meatballs in the air fryer for 10 to 12 minutes, or until they are completely cooked, turning halfway through (you may need to work in batches).

Air-Fryer Nashville Hot Chicken

Prep Time: 10 minutes

Cook Time: 15 minutes

Servings: 4

Ingredients

- 1 lb. of chicken tenders
- ¾ cup of panko breadcrumbs
- ¾ cup of milk
- 1 teaspoon of paprika
- 2 tablespoons of hot sauce
- ½ teaspoon of garlic powder
- Oil for spraying; Olive Oil, Canola, or any oil with a high smoke point
- ½ teaspoon of onion powder
- ½ teaspoon of Italian seasoning
- ½ teaspoon of salt
- Salt and pepper to taste
- ¼ teaspoon of black pepper

For Hot Paste

- 2 tablespoons of brown sugar

- ½ cup of peanut oil
- 1 teaspoon of garlic powder
- 1 ½ tablespoons of cayenne pepper
- 1 teaspoon of dry mustard
- ½ teaspoon of salt
- 1 teaspoon of paprika

Instructions

1. Season the chicken tenders with pepper and salt. Set aside. In one bowl, whisk together hot sauce and milk. In a separate bowl, mix onion powder, Italian seasoning, paprika, garlic powder, panko breadcrumbs, black pepper, and salt.
2. Preheat the air fryer to 375°F.
3. Coat chicken tenders in milk mixture, drain off the excess milk, then coat chicken in the breadcrumb mixture; making sure both sides are coated.
4. Put the chicken in a greased air fryer basket or a parchment sheet liner. Cook for 14 to 16 minutes at 375°F, or until chicken is thoroughly cooked; flipping, and spraying chicken halfway through cooking.
5. Meanwhile, make the hot paste. In a medium-sized saucepan over medium heat, add cayenne pepper, peanut oil, dry mustard, brown sugar, paprika, salt, and garlic powder. Remove the mixture from the heat once it begins to bubble and simmer.
6. Once chicken tenders are cooked, take them out from the air fryer and put them into a large bowl. Pour the hot paste over the chicken and toss to combine; make sure that the hot sauce is equally spread. Serve right away.

Notes

- Preheat your air fryer before putting your chicken tenders to ensure even cooking.
- In the air fryer basket, arrange the tenders in a single layer.

- If you like milder chicken, then reduce the amount of cayenne pepper.
- Refrigerate leftovers in an airtight container. Reheat them in the air fryer for 3 to 4 minutes at 400°F.

Air Fryer Chicken Caprese

Prep Time: 10 minutes

Cook Time: 15 minutes

Servings: 4

Ingredients

- 4 slices of fresh mozzarella cheese (4 ounces)
- 1 large tomato
- 4 chicken breast cutlets (about 1 pound)
- 1 teaspoon of Italian seasoning
- 1/2 teaspoon of pepper
- Basil and balsamic vinegar to garnish
- 1 teaspoon of salt

Instructions

1. Put the chicken breast cutlets on a plate and pat them dry with a paper towel. After that, season them with salt, pepper, and Italian seasoning.
2. Place them in the air fryer basket and cook for 10 minutes at 380°F. After 5 minutes, turn them over with tongs. Make sure the air fryer basket isn't overloaded with chicken; there should be enough space for the air to circulate.
3. Slice the tomato and cheese while the chicken is cooking.
4. When the air fryer is done, check the chicken with a thermometer to ensure it has reached 165° F. If it isn't done, put the chicken back in the air fryer for 1 or 2 minutes.

5. Take out the chicken from the air fryer and top each with a slice of mozzarella cheese and a tomato. To do this, use a fork or tongs, and be careful not to touch the basket's edges; they will be very hot.

6. Return the basket to the air fryer and melt the cheese for 1 minute at 200°F. After 1 minute, keep the basket closed for another minute. Take it out from the air fryer.

7. If desired, sprinkle basil and balsamic vinegar on top of the chicken. Serve immediately.

Notes

- In this recipe, fresh ripe tomatoes are essential. If tomatoes aren't in season, you can use cherry or grape tomatoes because they also have great flavor.
- If you use full-sized, boneless chicken breasts rather than chicken breast cutlets, increase the cooking time to 20 minutes.

Pretzel Chicken Cordon Bleu

Prep Time: 15 minutes

Cook Time: 30 minutes

Servings: 5

Ingredients

- 3 cups of pretzels
- 5 boneless, skinless chicken thighs (about 4.5 lbs.)
- Cooking spray
- 5 slices of Swiss cheese
- 10 slices of deli-style honey ham
- 2 eggs, beaten

Instructions

1. Preheat the air fryer to 375° F.

2. Remove any excess fat from the chicken thighs.

3. Put three cups of pretzels in a food processor. Pulse until the pretzels are finely powdered (about 5 to 10 seconds). Spread pretzel crumbs on a plate.

4. Add two eggs into a small bowl. Beat until the yoke and whites are fully combined.

5. Place the chicken on a cutting board or plate. Put one slice of Swiss cheese and two slices of ham over each chicken thigh. Then roll the chicken, so the cheese and the ham surround it. Use toothpicks to keep everything in place. Repeat the procedure with the remaining chicken thighs.

6. Dip the chicken thighs in the egg mixture. Dredge the chicken in the pretzel crumbs until a thin layer covers the outside of the chicken. Repeat the process with the remaining chicken thighs.

7. Gently spray the chicken with cooking oil and place it on the air fryer tray. Cook for 26 to 30 minutes in the air fryer, or until the chicken is thoroughly cooked.

8. Remove the chicken from the air fryer. Serve with salad.

Air Fryer Stuffed Chicken Breast

Prep Time: 10 minutes

Cook Time: 25 minutes

Servings: 1

Ingredients

- 1 boneless chicken breast
- 1 strip of bacon
- 2 toothpicks (optional)
- 2 slices of cheddar cheese
- 1/4 teaspoon of dry basil
- 1/4 teaspoon of salt
- Cooking spray

- 1/4 teaspoon of garlic powder
- 2 slices of tomato

Instructions

1. Make a pocket in the chicken breast by cutting horizontally with a sharp knife, be careful not to cut through the whole way.
2. Mix garlic powder, salt, and dry basil in a small bowl. Season the chicken on both sides evenly.
3. Stuff one slice of cheddar cheese, bacon, and tomato slices into the chicken breast, then top with another slice of cheddar cheese.
4. Close the pocket properly with toothpicks (optional).
5. Spray the chicken breasts with cooking spray. Coating the chicken breast in oil will make it crispier on the outside.
6. In the air fryer basket, arrange the chicken breasts (on top of the crisper plate if your air fryer has one). Preheat the air fryer to 350°F and set the timer for 25 minutes.
7. To check if the chicken is cooked thoroughly, use an instant-read thermometer. The temperature should be 165° F. If necessary, cook for another 3 to 5 minutes.

Air Fryer Chicken Parmesan

Prep Time: 15 minutes

Cook Time: 15 minutes

Servings: 4

Ingredients

- 1/4 cup of parmesan cheese, shredded
- 2 large boneless skinless chicken breasts, cut in half horizontally
- 1/2 cup of Italian breadcrumbs
- 1/2 cup of marinara sauce

- Salt and pepper, to taste
- 1 large egg, beaten
- 1 teaspoon of garlic powder
- 1/2 cup mozzarella cheese, shredded

Instructions

1. Preheat your air fryer to 360° F for 3-5 minutes.
2. Place the cut chicken breasts on a cutting board and cover them with parchment paper. Pound the chicken to an even thickness with a meat mallet or heavy rolling pin. Season with pepper and salt on both sides.
3. On a shallow plate, combine the parmesan, breadcrumbs, and garlic powder. Whisk the egg in a separate bowl. Dip the chicken breast in the egg mixture, then coat evenly in the breadcrumb mixture.
4. Lightly spray each chicken breast with non-stick spray for a crispier golden crust, then arrange in an even layer in the air fryer basket. If your air fryer is small, you might have to do this in batches.
5. Cook for 6 minutes at 360° F, then flip and cook for another 3 minutes.
6. Top each chicken breast with two tablespoons of marinara sauce and two tablespoons of mozzarella cheese, then continue cooking for an additional 3 minutes. Serve with pasta if desired.

Air Fryer Orange Chicken

Prep Time: 5 minutes

Cook Time: 15 minutes

Servings: 2

Ingredients

- 2 tablespoons of cornstarch or potato starch
- 1-pound boneless skinless chicken breasts or chicken thighs

For the Orange Sauce

- 1/2 cup of orange juice
- 1 tablespoon of rice wine vinegar
- 2 tablespoons of brown sugar
- Dash of red pepper flakes
- 1 tablespoon of soy sauce
- 1/4 teaspoon of ground ginger (or 1/2 teaspoon freshly grated ginger)
- Zest of one orange

Optional to Serve.

- Sesame seeds
- Green onions, chopped

Instructions

1. Preheat the air fryer to 400° F.
2. In a bowl, combine the cornstarch and chicken pieces, and stir until the chicken is finely coated.
3. Cook for 7 to 9 minutes, or until the chicken reaches an internal temperature of 165° F, shaking the basket halfway through.
4. Meanwhile, in a small saucepan over medium heat, mix the brown sugar, soy sauce, orange juice, red pepper flakes, ginger, orange zest, and rice wine vinegar.
5. Bring the mixture to a simmer and simmer for 5 minutes.
6. In a small bowl, mix water and cornstarch, then add it to the orange sauce.
7. Simmer for another minute while stirring, then remove from heat.
8. Take the chicken out of the air fryer and mix it with the sauce.
9. Top with sesame seeds and green onions if desired. Serve right away.

Notes

This will make enough sauce to coat the chicken. If you want extra sauce for a full stir fry, you can double the recipe.

Chicken Taquitos

Prep Time: 15 minutes

Cook Time: 10 minutes

Servings: 12

Ingredients

- 12 small corn or flour tortillas
- 4 ounces of cream cheese, softened
- ½ cup of salsa of choice
- Oil or cooking spray
- 3 cups of cooked shredded chicken
- 1 cup of shredded Mexican blend cheese or Monterey Jack or cheddar; or your favorite melting cheese
- Salt and pepper to taste
- 1 teaspoon of chili powder
- 1 teaspoon of garlic powder
- 1 teaspoon of cumin
- For topping (optional) sour-cream, cilantro, avocado, Guacamole, tomato, lime

Instructions

1. In a large bowl, combine the spices, shredded chicken, and cheeses.

2. Arrange the tortillas on a flat surface and divide the chicken and cheese mixture evenly among them. Roll up the tortillas tightly. Using a cooking spray or a brush, lightly layer oil on all sides of the tortillas.

3. Arrange the taquitos in a single layer in the air fryer, avoid overcrowding it. Air fry for 12-15 minutes at 400° F or until crisp. To avoid burning them, open the air fryer after 12 minutes to check on them.

Chapter 4: Air Fryer Meat Recipes

Air frying is generally better than frying in oil. It reduces calories from 80% to 70%. Here we have delightful meat recipes that you can make in your air fryer right now.

Air Fryer Steak Bites and Mushrooms

Prep Time: 10 minutes

Cook Time: 18 minutes

Servings: 3

Ingredients

- 2 tablespoons (about 30 ml) of butter, melted (or olive oil)
- 1-pound (454 g) of steaks, cut into 1/2-inch cubes (sirloin, ribeye, tri-tip or what you prefer)
- 1 teaspoon (5 ml) of Worcestershire sauce
- Melted butter, for finishing, optional
- 8 oz. (227 g) mushrooms (washed, cleaned, and halved)
- 1/2 teaspoon (about 2.5 ml) of garlic powder, optional
- Flakey salt, to taste

- Chili Flakes, for finishing, optional
- Fresh cracked black pepper, to taste
- Minced parsley for garnish

Instructions

1. Wash and pat dry the steak cubes with a paper towel. Combine the mushrooms and steak cubes in a bowl. Coat with melted butter and then season with salt, pepper, Worcestershire sauce, and garlic powder.
2. Preheat the Air Fryer for 4 minutes at 400°F.
3. In the air fryer basket, arrange the steak and mushrooms in an even layer. Air fry for 10-18 minutes at 400°F, shaking and tossing the steak and mushrooms twice during the cooking process (time depends on your size of air fryer, desired doneness, and the thickness of the steak).
4. Check the steak and see how well it is cooked. Cook the steak for an additional 2-5 minutes if you like it more cooked.
5. Garnish with parsley and drizzle with melted butter and chili flakes. If desired, season with more pepper and salt. Serve right away.

Notes

- This recipe was cooked in a 3–4-quart air fryer. If you use a larger air fryer, the recipe can cook faster, so change the cooking time accordingly.
- Set a timer to shake, flip, or toss the food as directed in the recipe.
- It is preferable to preheat the Air Fryer. If you don't preheat, the cooking time would be longer.

Roast Beef – with Herb Crust

Prep Time: 5 minutes

Cook Time: 1 hour

Additional Time: 10 minutes

Servings: 6

Ingredients

- 2 lb. of roast beef
- 2 teaspoons of garlic powder
- 2 teaspoons of onion salt
- 2 teaspoons of parsley
- 2 teaspoons of thyme
- 2 teaspoons of basil
- 1/2 tablespoon of salt
- 1 teaspoon of pepper
- 1 tablespoon of olive oil

Instructions

1. Preheat the air fryer to 390° F for 15 minutes. Combine the parsley, basil, garlic powder, onion salt, thyme, salt, and pepper in a bowl.
2. Rub the olive oil all over the roast, then rub the herb mixture all over the roast.
3. Place the roast in the air fryer basket. Set a 15-minute timer. Remove the basket after 15 minutes and flip the roast.
4. Return the roast to the air fryer and reduce the temperature to 360° F. Cook for further 60 minutes, or until the thermometer reaches the desired level of doneness. Allow 15 minutes for the roast to set before cutting.

Notes

- For this air fryer recipe, use a tender cut of meat. You can use ribeye, tenderloin, or top loin.
- Use foil to line your air fryer basket to catch drippings.
- To make cleaning the fryer basket easier, spray it with cooking spray.
- Preheat your air fryer to 390° F for 15 minutes before placing the roast in.

Air Fryer Beef and Bean Chimichangas

Prep Time: 15 minutes

Cook Time: 8 minutes

Servings: 10

Ingredients

- 10 Taco Size Flour Tortillas, or 5 Burrito Flour Size Tortillas
- 1 Pound of Ground Beef
- 1 Package of Taco Seasoning
- 1/2 Cup of Refried Beans
- 1/2 Cup of Shredded Colby Jack Cheese
- Toppings - Queso, Tomato, Lettuce, Salsa, Sour Cream

Instructions

1. Brown the ground beef and add the taco seasoning according to the package instructions.
2. When the meat is cooked, combine it with the refried beans.
3. Add the mixture into the tortillas' center and top with shredded cheese.
4. Fold the tortilla to ensure that all of the toppings are secure inside.
5. Spray non-stick cooking spray or olive oil spray on the air fryer.

6. Arrange the chimichangas in the air fryer seam side down.
7. Use olive oil spray to coat them.
8. Cook for 8 minutes at 360° F. Check on them after 5 minutes to make sure they're cooked.
9. When they're done, they should be lightly browned on top, and the tortilla should be nicely secure.

Notes

Note that each air fryer heats up differently, so check on these after the 5-minute mark to make sure they're cooking well. They will need to be cooked for 10 minutes in some air fryers. Since the filling is already prepared, the main step is to cook the tortilla.

Beef Steak Kabobs

Prep Time: 30 minutes

Cook Time: 10 minutes

Servings: 4

Ingredients

- 1/3 cup of low-fat sour cream
- 1 pound of beef chuck ribs, cut in 1-inch pieces or any other tender cut meat
- 1 bell pepper
- 1/2 onion
- 8 6-inch skewers
- 2 tablespoons of soy sauce

Instructions

1. In a medium bowl, combine the soy sauce and sour cream. Place the beef chunks in the bowl and leave to marinate for at least 30 minutes, preferably overnight.

2. Cut the onion and bell pepper into 1-inch pieces. Soak wooden skewers for about 10 minutes in water.
3. Thread the onions, bell peppers, and beef onto skewers. Sprinkle with freshly ground black pepper.
4. Cook for 10 minutes in a preheated air fryer at 400°F, turning halfway through.

Air Fryer Corned Beef Hash

Prep Time: 10 minutes

Cook Time: 15 minutes

Servings: 2

Ingredients

- 1/2 cup of onion, chopped
- 1 ½ cups of cooked corned beef, cubed
- 1 ½ cups of cooked potatoes, cut into cubes
- 1 to 2 tablespoons of bacon fat (or your preferred oil)

Instructions

1. Spray a pan with the non-stick cooking spray.
2. Add the bacon fat and the rest of the ingredients to the bottom of the pan. Stir all together.
3. Gently set the cake pan into the air fryer basket. Cook at 390° F for 10 minutes.
4. Take out the air fryer basket and place it on a potholder. In the hash mixture, make two wells.
5. Crack an egg into each well.
6. Return the basket to the air fryer and set it to 370° F. Cook for 3-4 minutes, depending on how cooked you like your eggs. If you like sunny-side up eggs, 3-4 minutes is ideal. To avoid overcooking the egg, check it every 30 seconds. The top of the egg will grow a white layer, but the yolk underneath will still be slightly runny.

7. Using a large spoon, scoop out the hash and egg, and serve with rye toast and fruit or tomatoes.

Air Fryer Meatballs

Prep Time: 15 minutes

Cook Time: 10 minutes

Servings: 5

Ingredients

- 1/2 lb. of ground pork
- 1 egg
- 1/2 lb. of ground beef
- 1/2 cup of finely shredded Parmesan cheese
- 2 tablespoons of water
- 1 slice of soft bread
- 1 teaspoon of Italian seasoning
- 1/4 teaspoon of pepper
- 1/2 teaspoon of salt

Instructions

1. Preheat the air fryer to 400° F.
2. Cut the bread into small pieces and put it in a food processor. Process until the bread is in fine crumbs and then combine with water. Stir and set aside for a few minutes.
3. Add the pork, beef, egg, soaked bread, Italian seasoning, pepper, and salt in a large bowl. Combine the ingredients, but don't over-mix.
4. Shape into 1.5-2-inch balls.

5. Spray your air fryer basket lightly with non-stick spray and fill it with meatballs, leaving 1/2 inch between them. You'll probably need to do it in few batches.

6. Cook at 400°F for 7-8 minutes, or until a meat thermometer inserted in the largest meatball measures a minimum of 160°F. If they aren't cooked, move them back to the air fryer and cook for a further 2 minutes.

7. Repeat until all of the meatballs are cooked, then serve.

Air Fryer Steak Fajitas

Prep Time: 10 minutes

Cook Time: 17 minutes

Servings: 4

Ingredients

- 1/2 red bell pepper sliced
- 1/2 green bell pepper sliced
- 1.5 lbs. of top sirloin or flank steak, sliced against the grain
- 1 onion, sliced
- 2 tablespoons of lime juice
- 1 tablespoon of olive oil
- 1 tablespoon of soy sauce
- ¼ cup of pineapple juice
- ½ teaspoon of smoked paprika
- 1 tablespoon of minced garlic
- 1 teaspoon of cumin
- Pepper and salt, to taste
- ½ tablespoon of chili powder

Instructions

1. Mix the lime juice, chili powder, pineapple juice, soy sauce, olive oil, minced garlic, cumin, and smoked paprika in a bowl. Pour over steak and allow to marinate for 2 to 4 hours in the refrigerator.
2. Place a piece of foil in the air fryer basket and place onions and peppers in the basket. Spray with oil, and season with pepper and salt.
3. Cook for 10 minutes at 400° F. Add steak pieces on top of peppers after 10 minutes. Cook for 7 minutes at 400° F, or until the steak is cooked to your desired taste.
4. Place on tortillas and serve. Top with your favorite toppings such as cilantro, cheese, salsa, sour cream, etc.

Beef Chips

Prep Time: 10 minutes

Cook Time: 1 hour

Servings: 2

Ingredients

- 1/2 pound of Thinly Sliced Beef; we recommend leaner cuts like round or sirloin
- 1/4 teaspoon of Salt
- 1/4 teaspoon of Black Pepper
- 1/4 teaspoon of Garlic Powder

Instructions

1. To make the seasoning, add the black pepper, salt, and garlic powder in a small bowl and stir well.
2. Lay the beef slices flat and season on both sides.
3. Place single-stacked beef slices in an air fryer tray and air fry for 45-60 minutes at 200°F (there must be enough space between each slice; otherwise, they won't get

crispy). Allow beef slices to cool for 5 minutes before serving. Note that the time can vary significantly depending on the thickness of the meat.

Air Fryer Meatloaf

Prep Time: 10 minutes

Cook Time: 25 minutes

Additional Time: 10 minutes

Servings: 4

Ingredients

- 1 egg, lightly beaten
- 1-pound of lean ground beef
- 2 mushrooms, thickly sliced
- 1 small onion, finely chopped
- ground black pepper, to taste
- 1 teaspoon of salt
- 1 tablespoon of chopped fresh thyme
- 3 tablespoons of dry breadcrumbs
- 1 tablespoon of olive oil, or as needed

Instructions

1. Preheat the air fryer to 392° F (200° C).
2. In a bowl, combine the breadcrumbs, thyme, onion, ground beef, egg, pepper, and salt. Knead and thoroughly combine the ingredients.
3. Smooth the surface of the beef mixture in a baking pan. Press the mushrooms on top and coat with olive oil. Place the pan in the air fryer basket and slide it into the air fryer.
4. Set the air fryer for 25 minutes and roast the meatloaf until nicely browned.

5. Allow at least 10 minutes for the meatloaf to rest before slicing into wedges and serving.

Crispy Roast Pork Belly

Prep Time: 30 minutes

Cook Time: 1 hour

Servings: 4

Ingredients

- 3 cups of water
- 1 kg of pork belly
- 1 teaspoon of sea salt
- 1 teaspoon of sugar

Skin Rub

- 1 teaspoon of sea salt
- 1/2 tablespoon of vinegar

Meat Rub

- 1/4 teaspoon of sea salt
- 1/4 teaspoon of Chinese 5 spice powder

Instructions

1. Remove hair on the pork skin with a knife if there is any. Then properly wash the pork belly.
2. Combine the water, sugar, and salt in a frying pan over medium-high heat.
3. Add the pork belly, skin side down, to the boiling water and cook for 8 minutes on each side.
4. Once done, take out the pork belly and let it cool on a rack. When it's cool enough to handle, pat dry with a paper towel.

5. Using a meat skewer, make several holes in the skin of the pork belly. Do not punch holes too deep that it reaches the meat.

6. Brush the pork skin with vinegar, and then sprinkle half the salt. Set aside for 10 minutes and repeat the process.

7. Refrigerate the pork belly, uncovered, for at least 12 hours to allow the skin to dry. If possible, check on it from time to time to clean away any moisture that comes to the surface.

8. Remove the pork belly from the fridge and apply the meat rub all over it, including the sides and bottom.

9. Preheat the air fryer for 5 minutes, then cook the pork belly at 392° F (200° C) for 40 minutes.

10. Once cooked, set it aside for 15 minutes before cutting.

Air Fryer Pork Tenderloin

Prep Time: 5 minutes

Cook Time: 20 minutes

Servings: 2

Ingredients

- 1 pound of pork tenderloin
- 1 tablespoon of Dijon mustard
- 4 garlic cloves, minced
- 1/4 teaspoon of kosher salt and black pepper
- 1 tablespoon of fresh rosemary leaves, chopped

Instructions

1. Preheat the air fryer to 400°F. Score the pork tenderloin (cut small slits in the top, about 3/4 inch apart). Combine the rosemary leaves, Dijon mustard, minced garlic, black pepper, and kosher salt (to taste) in a small bowl. Spread

the garlic rosemary mixture over the pork tenderloin, making sure it spreads in all of the little cuts.

2. Cook the tenderloin (you may need to cut it in half to fit) in the air fryer for about 20 minutes, or until it reaches an internal temperature of 145° F. Slice, and serve warm.

Air Fryer Tonkatsu

Prep Time: 10 minutes

Cook Time: 20 minutes

Servings: 4

Ingredients

For Pork

- 2 large eggs
- 1 ½ cups of panko breadcrumbs
- 1 lb. of boneless pork breakfast chops (4 chops)
- Non-stick cooking spray
- Salt and ground black pepper, to taste

For Tonkatsu Sauce

- 2 tablespoons of soy sauce
- 2 teaspoons of Worcestershire sauce
- 1 tablespoon of brown sugar
- 1 teaspoon of minced garlic
- 1 tablespoon of sherry
- ½ cup of ketchup

Instructions

1. In a bowl, add the Worcestershire sauce, soy sauce, ketchup, garlic, sherry, and brown sugar; mix until all the sugar dissolved. Set aside the tonkatsu sauce.

2. Preheat your air fryer to 350°F (175° C).

3. Season the pork chops with pepper and salt.

4. In a flat dish, whisk together the eggs. Place the breadcrumbs in a separate flat dish. Dredge the pork chops in eggs, then in breadcrumbs. Repeat, dredging them in egg and then breadcrumbs again, pressing down so that the breadcrumbs stick to the chops.

5. Arrange pork chops in the preheated air fryer basket and spray the tops with non-stick cooking spray. Cook for 10 minutes. With a spatula, flip the chops and spray the tops with non-stick cooking spray once more. Cook for a further 10 minutes.

6. Once cooked, transfer to a cutting board and slice. Serve with tonkatsu sauce.

Air-Fryer Ground Beef Wellington

Prep Time: 30 minutes

Cook Time: 20 minutes

Servings: 2

Ingredients

- 1/2-pound of ground beef
- 1/4 teaspoon of pepper, divided
- 1 large egg yolk
- 2 teaspoons of all-purpose flour
- 1/2 cup of chopped fresh mushrooms
- 2 tablespoons of finely chopped onion
- 1 tube (4 ounces) refrigerated crescent rolls

- 1 large egg, lightly beaten, optional
- 1 tablespoon of butter
- 1 teaspoon of dried parsley flakes
- 1/2 cup of half-and-half cream
- 1/4 teaspoon of salt

Instructions

1. Preheat the air fryer to 300° F.

2. Melt butter in a saucepan over medium-high heat. Add mushrooms, cook, and stir until tender, about 5-6 minutes. Add the flour and 1/8 teaspoon pepper, stir well. Gradually add cream. Bring to a boil, cook, and stir for 2 minutes, or until thickened. Take the pan off the heat and set it aside.

3. Combine the onion, two tablespoons of mushroom sauce, salt, egg yolk, and 1/8 teaspoon pepper in a bowl. Crumble beef over mixture and mix thoroughly. Shape into two loaves. Unroll the crescent dough and cut it into two rectangles, press perforations to seal. Place the meatloaf in each rectangle. Pinch the edges together to seal them. Brush with a beaten egg, if desired.

4. Place Wellingtons in a single layer on a greased tray in the air-fryer basket. Cook for 18 to 22 minutes, or until golden brown and a thermometer inserted into the meatloaf reads 160° F.

5. Meanwhile, warm the remaining sauce over low heat and add the parsley. Serve Wellingtons with sauce.

Beef Satay

Prep Time: 5 minutes

Cook Time: 10 minutes

Servings: 2

Ingredients

- 2 tablespoons of oil
- 1 tablespoon of Soy Sauce
- 1 lb. of beef flank steak, thinly slice them into long strips
- 1 tablespoon of minced ginger
- 1 teaspoon of ground coriander
- 1 tablespoon of minced garlic
- 1/2 cup of chopped cilantro, divided
- 1 teaspoon of Sriracha sauce
- 1 tablespoon of fish sauce
- 1 tablespoon of sugar, or other sweetener equivalent
- 1/4 cup of roasted peanuts, chopped

Instructions

1. Place the beef strips in a large bowl or Ziplock bag.
2. Add the sugar, oil, soy sauce, 1/4 cup cilantro, garlic, Sriracha, ginger, fish sauce, and coriander to the beef and mix well. Marinate for at least 30 minutes, or up to 24 hours in the refrigerator.
3. Place the beef strips in the air fryer basket using tongs, laying them side by side and avoiding overlap.
4. Leave behind as much of the marinade as possible and discard this marinade.
5. Preheat your air fryer to 400°F and cook for 8 minutes, flipping halfway through.

6. Transfer the beef to a serving plate and top with chopped roasted peanuts and the remaining 1/4 cup cilantro.
7. Serve with easy peanut sauce.

Air Fryer Mongolian Beef

Prep Time: 20 minutes

Cook Time: 20 minutes

Servings: 4

Ingredients

Meat

- 1/4 cup of corn starch
- 1 pound of flank steak

Sauce

- 1 tablespoon of minced garlic
- 1/2 teaspoon of ginger
- 1/2 cup of water
- 2 teaspoons of vegetable oil
- 1/2 cup of Soy sauce, or gluten-free Soy sauce
- 3/4 cup of brown sugar, Packed

To Serve

- Green beans
- Green onions
- Cooked rice

Instructions

1. Slice the steak thinly into long pieces and coat them with corn starch.

2. Place in the air fryer and cook for 5 minutes on each side at 390°F. Start with 5 minutes and increase the time if required.

3. Warm all sauce ingredients in a medium-sized saucepan over medium-high heat while the steak cooks.

4. Mix the ingredients until it gets to a low boil.

5. Once both the steak and sauce are cooked, combine them in a bowl and let the sauce soak in for about 5-10 minutes.

6. To serve, remove the steak with tongs and let the excess sauce drip off.

7. Place steak on cooked rice and green beans, and top with more sauce if desired.

Lamb Chops

Prep Time: 10 minutes

Cook Time: 10 minutes

Servings: 4

Ingredients

- 1.5 lbs. of lamb loin chops/lamb leg chops

Marinade

- 1 teaspoon of dried rosemary
- ½ teaspoon of dried oregano
- ½ teaspoon of kosher salt
- ¼ teaspoon of black pepper
- 2 tablespoons of olive oil
- 1 tablespoon of red wine vinegar
- ½ teaspoon of garlic powder

Instructions

1. In a bowl, combine the red wine vinegar, olive oil, lamb chops, garlic powder, rosemary, oregano, black pepper, and salt. Rub the marinade into the lamb chops and cover, refrigerate for 1 hour.

2. Preheat the air fryer to 400°F.

3. Place the lamb chops in the air fryer basket and cook for about 7-9 minutes, or until they are cook to your desired doneness, flipping halfway through.

Notes

- For a medium-well cook, the lamb should reach an internal temperature of 145° F.
- Serve lamb chops with homemade chimichurri sauce.

Air Fryer Baby Back Ribs

Prep Time: 15 minutes

Cook Time: 35 minutes

Servings: 4

Ingredients

- 1 tablespoon of olive oil
- 1 cup of BBQ sauce
- 1 rack of baby back ribs
- ½ teaspoon of chili powder
- 1 tablespoon of brown sugar
- ½ teaspoon of garlic powder
- ½ teaspoon of salt
- 1 tablespoon of liquid smoke flavoring
- ½ teaspoon of onion powder
- ½ teaspoon of ground black pepper

Instructions

1. Remove membrane from the back of ribs and dry the ribs. Cut the rack into four pieces with a knife. In a small bowl, mix liquid smoke and olive oil, and rub on both sides of the ribs.

2. In a bowl, combine the garlic powder, chili powder, brown sugar, pepper, onion powder, and salt. Rub the seasoning mix on both sides of the ribs. Set aside for 30 minutes to enhance the flavor.

3. Preheat your air fryer to 375°F (190° C).

4. Place the ribs bone-side down in the air fryer basket, making sure they don't touch; if required, cook in batches.

5. Cook for 15 minutes. Cook for another 10 minutes after flipping the ribs (meat-side down). Remove the ribs from the air fryer and brush 1/2 cup BBQ sauce on the ribs' bone-side. Return the basket to the air fryer and cook for another 5 minutes. Flip the ribs, brush meat-side with 1/2 cup BBQ sauce; cook for an additional 5 minutes or until desired char is achieved.

Stuffed Peppers

Prep Time: 15 minutes

Cook Time: 15 minutes

Servings: 6

Ingredients

- 1 lb. of lean ground beef
- 6 green bell peppers
- 1/4 cup of green onion, diced
- 1 tablespoon of olive oil
- 1/4 cup of fresh parsley
- 1/4 cup of shredded Mozzarella cheese

- 1/2 teaspoon of garlic salt
- 1 cup of Marinara Sauce, to taste
- 1 cup of cooked rice
- 1/2 teaspoon of ground sage

Instructions

1. Cook the ground beef in a medium-sized skillet until it is well done.
2. Drain the beef and return to the pan.
3. Add the parsley, olive oil, green onion, salt, and sage. Mix well.
4. Add marinara and cooked rice in the pan and mix thoroughly.
5. Remove the tops of each pepper and clean out the seeds.
6. Scoop the mixture into each pepper and arrange it in the air fryer basket.
7. Cook for 10 minutes at 355°F, then carefully open and sprinkle with cheese.
8. Cook for another 5 minutes, or until the peppers are softened and the cheese has melted.
9. Serve warm.

Turkey Burgers with Zucchini

Prep Time: 10 minutes

Cook Time: 10 minutes

Servings: 5

Ingredients

- 1 pound of 93% lean ground turkey
- Oil spray
- 1/4 cup of seasoned whole wheat, or gluten-free breadcrumbs
- 1 teaspoon of kosher salt and fresh pepper

- 1 garlic clove, grated
- 6 ounces of grated zucchini, when squeezed 4.25 oz
- 1 tablespoon of red onion, grated

Instructions

1. Use paper towels to squeeze out all the moisture from the zucchini.
2. Combine the breadcrumbs, zucchini, ground turkey, onion, garlic, pepper, and salt in a large bowl. Make five equal patties, about 1/2 inch thick.
3. Preheat the air fryer to 370° F.
4. Place in a single layer in the air fryer basket and cook for 10 minutes, until browned and cooked through in the center, turning halfway through.

Low-Carb Air Fryer Scotch Eggs

Prep Time: 15 minutes

Cook Time: 15 minutes

Servings: 6

Ingredients

- 5-6 hard-boiled eggs, peeled
- 1 pound (454 g) of uncooked bulk sausage
- Mustard or hot sauce
- Oil spray for coating
- 1-2 raw eggs, beaten
- 1 cup (480 ml) of coating of choice (almond flour, crushed pork rinds, coconut flour, or preferred coating; see notes below)

Instructions

1. Depending on how thick you want the sausage to wrap around the egg, divide it into 5 or 6 equal parts.

2. Shape each portion into a thin, 4-inch patty. Place a boiled egg in the center and wrap the sausage around it fully. Repeat with the remaining eggs.

3. Dip the sausage-wrapped egg in the beaten egg, then in the breading. Uniformly spray the outside of coated egg with oil.

4. Air fry for 12 to16 minutes at 400°F, turning halfway through. The thicker the sausage layer, the longer it takes to cook.

5. Slice in half and serve with hot sauce.

Notes

- By adding fresh parsley, Worcestershire sauce, and other spices to your sausage, you can enhance its flavor. If not, simple bulk sausage is always delicious! Panko flakes, breadcrumbs, or crushed crackers work well as breading options. Make sure to spray the outside of the sausage with oil.

Chapter 5: Air Fryer Fish and Seafood Recipes

These incredible air fryer fish recipes will take your seafood night to the next level. When you use the right seasonings, you'll be amazed by how much flavor you can get from these seafood dishes.

Zesty Ranch Air Fryer Fish Fillets

Prep Time: 5 minutes

Cook Time: 12 minutes

Servings: 4

Ingredients

- 4 tilapia salmon, or other fish fillets
- 1 packet of dry ranch-style dressing mix (30g)
- 2 eggs, beaten
- 3/4 cup of breadcrumbs or Panko or crushed cornflakes
- Lemon wedges, to garnish
- 2 1/2 tablespoons of vegetable oil

Instructions

1. Preheat your air fryer to 350° F.

2. Mix the ranch dressing and panko/breadcrumbs. Add the oil and keep mixing until the mixture is loose and crumbly.
3. Dip the fish fillets into the egg and drip off the excess.
4. Dredge the fish fillets in the crumb mixture, coating them uniformly and thoroughly.
5. Gently place in your air fryer.
6. Cook for about 12 to 13 minutes, depending on the thickness of the fillets.
7. Take out from the air fryer once done and serve. If desired, squeeze lemon wedges over the fish.

Air Fryer Catfish with Spicy Tartar Sauce

Prep Time: 5 minutes

Cook Time: 20 minutes

Servings: 4

Ingredients

Cajun Catfish

- 4 catfish fillets
- 3/4 cup of cornmeal
- 3 teaspoons of Cajun seasoning

Spicy Tartar Sauce

- 1/2 cup of mayonnaise
- 1 teaspoon of Cajun seasoning
- 1 tablespoon of lemon juice
- 1/4 cup of dill pickles

Instructions

For Cajun Catfish

1. In a gallon size Ziploc bag, combine the Cajun seasoning and cornmeal.
2. With paper towels, dry the catfish fillets. Then, two at a time, add them to the bag and shake to coat the fillets in the mixture. Repeat with the remaining fillets until they are all coated.
3. In the air fryer basket, arrange the catfish fillets. Make sure there is enough space between them.
4. Cook for 15 minutes at 390°F, flipping the fillets halfway through.
5. Raise the temperature to 400° F and cook for a further 5 minutes to brown the fillets nicely.
6. Serve with spicy tartar sauce and lemon wedges.

For Spicy Tartar Sauce

1. Chop the dill pickles into small pieces.
2. Mix the dill pickles, Cajun seasoning, mayonnaise, and lemon juice in a bowl.

Fried Shrimp

Prep Time: 10 minutes

Cook Time: 10 minutes

Servings: 4

Ingredients

- 1 pound of peeled and deveined raw shrimp
- 2 teaspoons of black pepper, divided
- 1 cup of panko breadcrumbs
- 2 large eggs, beaten
- 1/2 cup of all-purpose flour

- Canola oil cooking spray (or any non-stick spray)
- Store-bought remoulade sauce
- 2 teaspoons of kosher salt, divided
- 1 teaspoon of paprika, divided

Instructions

1. Arrange three shallow bowls. Add 1 teaspoon black pepper, flour, 1 teaspoon salt, and 1/2 teaspoon paprika to the first one. Stir with a fork until everything is well combined.

2. In the second bowl, whisk together two eggs. In the third bowl, add the panko, 1 teaspoon salt, 1 teaspoon black pepper, and 1/2 teaspoon paprika. To mix, use a fork to stir it together.

3. Dry the shrimp with a paper towel and then coat in the flour mixture, then dip in the eggs, and lastly, coat with the panko mixture. Set aside on a plate and repeat with the remaining shrimp.

4. Preheat the air fryer to 390° F. In the bottom of the air fryer basket, layer the breaded shrimp in a single layer. Lightly spray with a canola oil cooking spray, then cook for 5 minutes.

5. Shake the basket, lightly spray with oil, and cook for a further 5 minutes, or until the shrimp are golden brown.

6. Serve right away with dipping sauces of your choice.

Notes

1. If you're using frozen shrimp, make sure they're fully thawed and dry.

2. If you want to make more shrimp, cook them in batches, so they cook evenly. If you stack them on top of each other, they will steam and not crisp up as well.

Air Fryer Fish Sticks

Prep Time: 10 minutes

Cook Time: 12 minutes

Servings: 4

Ingredients

- 1 pound of cod fish fillet
- Cooking oil spray
- 2 eggs
- ½ teaspoon of kosher salt

Flour Mixture

- 1/2 teaspoons of kosher salt, divided
- ½ teaspoon of black pepper, freshly ground
- ½ teaspoon of cayenne pepper
- ½ teaspoon of garlic powder
- ½ cup of all-purpose flour
- ½ teaspoon of paprika

Breadcrumb's mixture

- ½ teaspoon of kosher salt
- ½ teaspoon of black pepper, freshly ground
- ½ cup of unseasoned breadcrumbs, or panko

Sauce

- 1/3 cup of mayonnaise
- 2 tablespoons of sriracha hot chili sauce

Instructions

1. Wash and pat dry the fish fillet. Cut each piece into 4-inch x 1-inch-long pieces. You may end up with 6 to 10 pieces based on the thickness of the fish. Sprinkle and rub 1/2 teaspoon of salt all over the fish pieces.

2. Beat the eggs in a large bowl.

3. Mix all the flour mixture in another large bowl.

4. Mix the pepper, salt, breadcrumbs in a third large bowl.

5. Dip one fish piece into the flour mixture, make sure it's properly coated on both sides. Pick up the fish and gently put it in the egg mixture. Uniformly cover the fish with the egg and put it in the breadcrumb bowl. Using a dry hand, coat the fish in breadcrumbs. Repeat with the remaining fish fillets.

6. Spray the cooking oil into the air fryer basket. Gently place the coated fish in the basket, make sure there is enough space between them. Apply a light spray of oil on top. Set the temperature to 400° F and cook for 8 minutes. Then flip the fish, gently spray with oil, and cook for another 4 minutes, or until the fish is flaky when cut with a fork. You may also use a digital thermometer to ensure that the thickest part's internal temperature is 145°.

To Serve

1. Serve with Sriracha Mayo. To make the mayo, whisk sriracha sauce with mayo.

2. You can also serve the fish fingers with tartar sauce by mixing two tablespoons of finely diced pickles, 1/2 tablespoon of lemon juice, 1/3 cup of mayo, and one tablespoon of fresh dill or parsley. Add salt & pepper to taste.

Air Fryer Garlic Butter Salmon

Prep Time: 5 minutes

Cook Time: 10 minutes

Servings: 2

Ingredients

- 2 tablespoons of butter, melted
- 2 (about 6-ounces) of boneless, skin-on salmon fillets (preferably wild-caught)
- 1 teaspoon of garlic, minced
- Salt and pepper, to taste
- 1 teaspoon of fresh Italian parsley, chopped (or 1/4 teaspoon dried)

Instructions

1. Heat the air fryer to 360° F.
2. Season the fresh salmon with pepper and salt, then combine the parsley, melted butter, and garlic in a bowl.
3. Rub the butter garlic mixture on the salmon fillets and gently place them side by side in the air fryer, skin side down.
4. Cook for about 10 minutes, or until the salmon easily flakes with a fork or knife.
5. Serve right away.

Notes

How to reheat salmon in an air fryer?

- Cook the salmon for 4 minutes in a preheated air fryer set to 370° F.

How to cook frozen salmon fillet in an air fryer?

- To thaw frozen salmon fillets, cook them skin side down in a preheated air fryer at 390° F for about 4 minutes, or until the salmon easily flakes with a fork or knife.

Air Fryer Cod with Lemon and Dill

Prep Time: 10 minutes

Cook Time: 20 minutes

Servings: 4

Ingredients

- 4 tablespoons of butter, melted
- 4 cod loins
- 6 cloves of garlic, minced
- 2 tablespoons of lemon juice (1 lemon)
- 1/2 teaspoon of salt
- 1 teaspoon of dried dill (or 2 tablespoons of fresh dill, chopped)

Instructions

1. Preheat the air fryer to 370° F.
2. In a bowl, mix the lemon juice, dill, butter, garlic, and salt.
3. Put a cod loin in the bowl and completely coat it. To avoid the garlic from falling off during cooking, lightly press it into the cod. Repeat with the remaining cod pieces.
4. Arrange the cod loins in a single layer in the air fryer, not touching each other.
5. Cook for 10 minutes in the air fryer.
6. Serve the cod with butter or more lemon juice, if desired.

Air Fryer Shrimp with Lemon and Pepper

Prep Time: 5 minutes

Cook Time: 10 minutes

Servings: 4

Ingredients

- 1-pound of medium raw shrimp, peeled and deveined
- 2 tablespoons of lemon juice
- 1/2 cup of olive oil
- 1/2 teaspoon of salt
- 1 teaspoon of black pepper

Optional

- 8 ounces of pasta, cooked per directions

Instructions

1. Preheat the air fryer to 400° F.
2. Combine the shrimp, lemon juice, olive oil, pepper, and salt in a Ziploc bag. Gently combine all ingredients.
3. Place parchment paper in the air fryer basket and put the raw shrimp in one layer.
4. Cook for 8 minutes, shaking the basket halfway through the cooking time. When the shells turn pink, and the shrimp is slightly white but still opaque, the shrimp is cooked.
5. Take out the lemon pepper shrimp from the air fryer and serve with pasta, if desired.

Notes

How to cook frozen raw shrimp in the air fryer?

1. Preheat your air fryer to 400° F.
2. Cook frozen, raw shrimp for about 8-10 minutes in an air fryer, shaking the basket halfway through.

3. Take the shrimp out of the air fryer and serve.
4. If you are using precooked frozen shrimp, then cook for about 5 minutes in the air fryer until warmed through.

How to reheat shrimp in the air fryer?

1. Preheat the air fryer to 350° F.
2. Cook the shrimp in the air fryer for 2-3 minutes, or until warmed.
3. Take the shrimp out of the air fryer and serve.

Tuna Steaks

Prep Time: 20 minutes

Cook Time: 5 minutes

Servings: 2

Ingredients

- 2 boneless and skinless yellowfin tuna steaks (about 6 ounces)
- 1 teaspoon of grated ginger
- 1 teaspoon of sesame oil
- 1/2 teaspoon of rice vinegar
- 2 teaspoons of honey
- 1/4 cup of soy sauce

Optional for Serving:

- Sesame seeds
- Green onions, sliced

Instructions

1. Take out the tuna steaks from the fridge.

2. Add the grated ginger, soy sauce, honey, rice vinegar, and sesame oil to a large bowl.

3. Put tuna steaks in the marinade and leave to marinate for about 20 to 30 minutes covered in the fridge.

4. Preheat the air fryer to 380° F and cook the tuna steaks in one layer for 4 minutes. Take out the tuna steaks from the air fryer once cooked to your desired doneness.

5. Allow the air fryer tuna steaks to rest for a minute before slicing and serving. If desired, garnish with sesame seeds and green onions.

Fish Nuggets

Prep Time: 10 minutes

Cook Time: 12 minutes

Servings: 2

Ingredients

- Non-stick cooking spray
- 1 lb. of catfish fillets, cut into 1-inch pieces
- 3/4 cup of seasoned fish fry coating

Instructions

1. Preheat the air fryer to 400° F.

2. Put seasoned breading mix in a plastic resealable bag. Place the catfish pieces in it, close the bag, and shake to coat the fish on all sides with breading.

3. Arrange the catfish nuggets on a baking sheet and gently spray with non-stick cooking spray. Place the nuggets in the air fryer basket in an even layer, sprayed side down. Spray the tops of nuggets with cooking spray.

4. Cook for 8 minutes in the air fryer. Flip the nuggets with tongs and cook for further 4 minutes.

Pesto Walnut Fish Fillets

Prep Time: 10 minutes

Cook time: 10 minutes

Servings: 2

Ingredients

- 2 6oz cod fillets (about 170g each) defrosted and patted dry with a paper towel
- 2 tablespoons of pesto sauce
- 2 tablespoons of grated parmesan cheese (optional)
- 1/4 cup of chopped walnuts
- Salt and pepper, to taste
- 1 tablespoon of mayonnaise

Instructions

1. Line the air fryer basket with a sheet of lightly greased aluminum foil or grill mat.
2. Mix the mayonnaise, pesto sauce, pepper, and salt in a small bowl.
3. Arrange the fish fillets in the fryer basket. On each piece of fish, spread half of the pesto mixture and top with chopped walnuts.
4. Air fry for about 8 to 10 minutes at 380°F (190°C) until the fish is flaky and the internal temperature exceeds 145°F (63C).
5. Sprinkle parmesan cheese and serve.

Bacon-Wrapped Shrimp

Prep Time: 15 minutes

Cook Time: 10 minutes

Servings: 6

Ingredients

- 8 slices of center cut bacon
- 8 oz large shrimp thawed, peeled, deveined, and tail-off
- 1 teaspoon of Cajun seasoning blend
- 1 tablespoon of olive oil

Instructions

1. Toss the shrimp with seasoning and oil in a bowl.
2. Cut bacon slices in half lengthwise and then in half widthwise.
3. Wrap one slice of bacon around each shrimp piece and arrange seam side down in the air fryer in a single layer.
4. Cook for 6 to 8 minutes in an air fryer at 370°F, until the bacon is slightly crispy and shrimp is cooked through, turning once.

Low Carb Tuna Casserole

Prep Time: 10 minutes

Cook Time: 5 minutes

Servings: 2

Ingredients

- 1/4 cup of shredded cheese Mexican blend
- 2 5oz cans tuna in water, drained and fluffed (total about 280g)
- 1 tablespoon of Parmesan cheese

- 1/4 cup of onion, chopped
- 2 tablespoons of mayonnaise
- 1/4 teaspoon of cayenne pepper, or to taste
- 1/4 cup of finely chopped celery
- 1/4 teaspoon of salt
- 1/4 teaspoon of black pepper
- 1/4 teaspoon of onion powder
- 1/4 cup of Japanese panko, optional
- 2 tablespoons of chopped pickled jalapeno, optional
- Some thinly sliced green onion to garnish

Instructions

1. Lightly grease a 6-inch pizza pan.
2. Add all the ingredients, except the green onion, to a large bowl and stir well.
3. Put the mixture in the pizza pan and air fry for 5-6 minutes at 380° F (190°C) cook properly, when there are about 2 minutes left on the air fryer, top with extra cheese, if desired.
4. Garnish with some green onion and serve right away.

Air-Fryer Fish Cakes

Prep Time: 10 minutes

Cook Time: 20 minutes

Servings: 2

Ingredients

- 10 ounces of finely chopped white fish (such as cod or catfish)
- Non-stick cooking spray

- 1 large egg
- 2/3 cup of whole-wheat panko breadcrumbs
- 3 tablespoons of finely chopped fresh cilantro
- 2 tablespoons of Thai sweet chili sauce
- 2 tablespoons of canola mayonnaise
- 1/4 teaspoon of ground pepper
- 1/8 teaspoon of salt
- 2 lime wedges

Instructions

1. Spray the air fryer basket with non-stick cooking spray.
2. In a medium bowl, whisk together the egg, panko, fish, cilantro, mayonnaise, chili sauce, pepper, and salt. Make four 3-inch-diameter cakes from the mixture.
3. With cooking spray, spray the cakes and put them in the prepared basket. Cook at 400°F for about 9 to 10 minutes, or until the cakes are golden brown and their internal temperature reaches 140°F. Serve with lime wedges.

Air-Fryer Scallops with Lemon-Herb Sauce

Prep Time: 10 minutes

Cook Time: 10 minutes

Servings: 2

Ingredients

- 8 large (1-oz.) sea scallops, cleaned and patted very dry
- Cooking spray
- 2 tablespoons of finely chopped flat-leaf parsley
- 1/2 teaspoon of finely chopped garlic

- 1 teaspoon of finely grated lemon zest
- 1/8 teaspoon of salt
- 2 teaspoons of capers, finely chopped
- 1/4 teaspoon of ground pepper
- 1/4 cup of extra-virgin olive oil
- Lemon wedges, optional

Instructions

1. Season the scallops with salt and pepper. Grease the air fryer basket with cooking spray. Arrange scallops in the basket and coat them with cooking spray. Place the basket in the fryer. Cook the scallops at 400°F for about 6 minutes, or until they reach an internal temperature of 120°F.
2. In a small bowl, combine parsley, capers, garlic, oil, and lemon zest. Drizzle all over the scallops. If desired, serve with lemon wedges.

Air Fryer Bang Bang Shrimp

Prep Time: 10 minutes

Cook Time: 30 minutes

Servings: 6

Ingredients

For the shrimp

- 1 cup of cornstarch seasoned with salt and pepper
- 2 pounds of shrimp, peeled and deveined
- ½ to 1 cup of buttermilk
- Cooking oil spray
- 1 large egg whisked with 1 of teaspoon water

For the sauce

- 1/3 cup of sweet Thai chile sauce
- ¼ cup of sour cream
- ¼ cup of mayonnaise
- 2 tablespoons of buttermilk
- 1 tablespoon of sriracha, or to taste.
- Pinch of dried dill weed

Instructions

1. Add the corn starch to a wide, shallow bowl and season with salt and pepper.
2. Coat the shrimp in buttermilk.
3. Dredge the shrimp in the seasoned corn starch and place in the air fryer basket in a single layer. The shrimp may need to be cooked in batches.
4. Spray with cooking oil and brush all over with the egg wash.
5. Cook for 5 minutes at 400°F, until browned and crisp on top. Turn the shrimp over gently, spray with oil again, and brush with egg wash. On the second side, cook for 4 to 5 minutes, or until crispy and browned. Repeat with the rest of the shrimp.
6. Make the sauce. Whisk together the mayonnaise, sour cream, sweet chili sauce, dried dill weed, buttermilk, and sriracha, in a medium bowl and mix until smooth and well combined.
7. Drizzle the sauce over the shrimp or serve it on the side for dipping.

Notes

- If you don't have buttermilk, you can make your own at home by combining 1 teaspoon of lemon juice or distilled vinegar with 1 cup of regular milk and set aside the mixture for about five minutes.

Cheesy Egg and Tuna Bake

Prep Time: 10 minutes

Cook Time: 10 minutes

Servings: 2

Ingredients

- 2 (5 oz) canned tuna, drained and fluffed
- 1 egg
- 1/4 cup of panko breadcrumbs
- 1/3 cup of mozzarella cheese
- 1/3 cup of diced celery, or vegetable of your choice
- 3 tablespoons of mayonnaise
- 1 teaspoon of sriracha hot sauce
- 2 tablespoons of scallion for garnish, optional

Instructions

1. Lightly grease shallow bakeware and set it aside.
2. Combine all the ingredients, except the egg, in a large bowl. Then, pour the mixture into the bakeware. Lightly press the center of the mixture with a spoon and create a crater.
3. Crack an egg into the crater. Then air fry for about 8 to 10 minutes at 380° F (190°C), or until the egg white is completely cooked to your desired doneness.
4. To serve, sprinkle some scallion over the tuna bake.

Chapter 6: Air Fryer Vegetable Recipes

One of the most common misconceptions about air fryers, is that they are only used to reheat frozen foods. However, the air fryer is capable of far more than just reheating frozen foods. Here are some healthy vegetable recipes that will make air frying one of your favorite ways to cook and prepare meals!

Air Fryer Roasted Cauliflower

Prep Time: 5 minutes

Cook Time: 10 minutes

Servings: 8

Ingredients

- Olive oil cooking spray
- 1 head of cauliflower
- 1 teaspoon of garlic salt

Instructions

1. Cut the cauliflower into small thin pieces.
2. Coat the air fryer basket with olive oil cooking spray and put the cauliflower in it.

3. Evenly coat with garlic salt and apply a second coat of olive oil cooking spray.

4. Air fry at 355°F for 10 minutes, tossing after 7 minutes, re-coating with olive oil spray, and then continue cooking.

5. Serve.

Air-Fried Beet Chips

Prep Time: 15 minutes

Cook Time: 50 minutes

Servings: 4

Ingredients

- 2 teaspoons of canola oil
- 3/4 teaspoon of kosher salt
- 3 medium red beets (1 1/2 pound), peeled and cut with a mandoline, about 1/8-inch-thick slices
- 1/4 teaspoon of black pepper

Instructions

1. Use a mandoline to make wafer-thin slices of the beet. Don't overload the basket; air circulation is necessary for crispy chips.

2. In a large bowl, combine the beet slices, salt, pepper, and oil.

3. Put half of the beets in the air fryer basket and cook for about 25 to 30 minutes, or until crispy and dry, at 320° F, shaking the basket every 5 minutes. Repeat with the rest of the beets in the same way.

Air-Fryer Roasted Green Beans

Prep Time: 15 minutes

Cook Time: 20 minutes

Servings: 6

Ingredients

- 1/2-pound of fresh mushrooms, sliced
- 1 teaspoon of Italian seasoning
- 1/8 teaspoon of pepper
- 1-pound of fresh green beans, cut into two-inch pieces
- 1/4 teaspoon of salt
- 2 tablespoons of olive oil
- 1 small red onion, halved and thinly sliced

Instructions

8. Preheat the air fryer to 375° F. Combine all ingredients in a large bowl and toss to coat.
9. On a greased tray in the air fryer basket, arrange the vegetables. Cook for about 8 to 10 minutes, or until just tender. Toss the vegetables to redistribute; cook for another 8 to 10 minutes, or until browned.

Potato and Kale Nuggets

Prep Time: 25 minutes

Cook Time: 20 minutes

Servings: 4

Ingredients

- 1 teaspoon of extra-virgin olive oil or canola oil
- 4 cups of coarsely chopped kale

- Vegetable oil spray
- 2 cups of finely chopped potatoes
- 1/8 cup of almond milk
- 1/8 teaspoon of ground black pepper
- 1/4 teaspoon of sea salt
- 1 garlic clove, minced

Instructions

1. Peel and wash the potatoes, then place them in a large saucepan of boiling water. Cook for about 30 minutes, or until they are tender.
2. Heat the oil in a large skillet over medium-high heat. Add the garlic and cook until golden brown. Add the kale and cook for 2 to 3 minutes.
3. Put the cooked potatoes in a large bowl. Then add salt, pepper, and milk, and mash with a potato masher or fork. Combine the cooked kale with mashed potatoes. Preheat the air fryer for 5 minutes at 390°F.
4. Make 1-inch nuggets from the kale and potato mixture. Spritz the vegetable oil into the air fryer basket. Place the nuggets in the air fryer basket and cook for about 12 to 15 minutes, or until they golden brown, shake the basket halfway through.

Air-Fryer Acorn Squash Slices

Prep Time: 15 minutes

Cook Time: 15 minutes/batch

Servings: 6

Ingredients

- 1/2 cup of butter, softened
- 2/3 cup of packed brown sugar
- 2 medium acorn squash

Instructions

1. Preheat the air fryer to 350° F. Slice the squash in half lengthwise, remove and discard the seeds.
2. Cut each half crosswise into 1/2-inch slices; discard the ends. Arrange squash in a single layer on a greased tray in the air fryer basket. Cook for 5 minutes per side, or until just tender.
3. Mix the butter and sugar in a bowl and spread it over the squash. Cook for a further 3 minutes.

Air Fried Eggplant (Gluten-Free)

Prep Time: 10 minutes

Cook Time: 10 minutes

Servings: 6

Ingredients

- 1 Eggplant
- 1/4 cup of breadcrumbs or gluten-free breadcrumbs
- 2 Eggs, beaten
- Olive oil cooking spray
- 1/4 cup of grated Parmesan cheese
- 1/4 cup of all-purpose flour, or gluten-free flour
- 1 tablespoon of Italian seasoning

Instructions

1. Cut the eggplant into thin slices, about 1/8-inch, and set aside.
2. Crack the eggs in a bowl and beat them well to combine.
3. In another bowl, add the flour.
4. Then, in a third bowl, combine the seasoning, breadcrumbs, and cheese.

5. Dip each eggplant slice in flour and shake off the excess.

6. Dip it into the eggs and coat it in the bread crumb mixture.

7. Spray a sheet of foil with olive oil spray and place it in the air fryer basket. Make sure it is rolled up on the side to allow the air to circulate.

8. Put the eggplant in a single layer in the air fryer basket and cook for 8 minutes.

9. Apply another coat of spray on top of the eggplant.

10. Cook for 5 minutes at 390° F.

11. Turn the eggplant gently and spray it with olive oil spray.

12. Cook for a further 5 minutes.

13. Remove from the air fryer once cooked and serve.

Notes

It's essential to keep in mind that all air fryers heat up differently, which is why you should check it halfway through the cooking time.

BRUSSELS SPROUTS

Prep Time: 5 minutes

Cook Time: 10 minutes

Servings: 2

Ingredients

- Olive oil cooking spray
- 1 lb. of brussels sprouts, halved
- 1/2 teaspoon of garlic salt, or to taste

Instructions

1. Line the air fryer with a sheet of foil.

2. Put the brussels sprouts in the air fryer.

3. Season with salt and coat with olive oil spray.

4. Cook for 5 minutes at 355°F, then turn the brussels sprouts.
5. Cook for a further 5 minutes, or until the desired crispiness is obtained.

Vegetable Stuffed Potato Patties

Prep Time: 30 minutes

Cook Time: 15 minutes

Servings: 6

Ingredients

For Patties

- 2 large eggs
- 1/3 cup of traditional breadcrumbs
- 4 cups of mashed potatoes, skin removed. About 6-7 potatoes.
- 1 tablespoon of olive oil
- 1/2 teaspoon of ground pepper
- 1/2 teaspoon of salt
- Non-stick spray

For Filling

- 1/2 cup of diced green bell pepper
- 1 small zucchini, peeled and diced
- 1/2 cup of diced onion
- 1/2 cup of diced red bell pepper
- 1 tablespoon of olive oil
- 2 tablespoons of Parmesan cheese, grated
- 1/2 teaspoon of ground pepper
- 1/2 teaspoon of salt

Instructions

1. Peel and cut the potatoes, then boil them for 20 minutes, or until they are soft. Drain the water from potatoes and put them in a bowl. Use a potato masher to mash them. Set aside to cool.

2. Chop the red pepper, zucchini, green pepper, and onion.

3. Heat olive oil in a skillet over medium heat. Add the vegetables and cook for 5 minutes, or until they are tender. Remove the skillet from the heat. Stir in the salt, pepper, and Parmesan cheese, to the sautéed vegetables.

4. Add breadcrumbs, salt, pepper, breadcrumbs, and eggs to the mashed potatoes and mix until completely combined.

5. Shape the mashed potatoes into balls and gently press down to make flat patties, about ¼-inch-thick. The patties will be about 5 inches in diameter. Repeat until all of the patties are made. You'll need a total of 12; All the patties must be equal in size.

6. Spread about two tablespoons of the vegetable mixture on top of one patty. Then place another patty on top, forming a sandwich. Press both sides together, so there are no seams showing.

7. Brush the tops and bottoms of the patties with olive oil.

8. Lightly spray the air fryer basket with non-stick spray. Place patties in the basket gently. To avoid overcrowding the basket, you may need to cook them in several batches.

9. Cook for 15 minutes at 400°F, gently flipping halfway through. Repeat until all of the potato patties are cooked.

Notes

- Because different air fryer brands cook at different rates, keep an eye on the food.

Air Fryer Onion Rings

Prep Time: 15 minutes

Cook Time: 12 minutes

Servings: 2

Ingredients

- 1 cup of panko breadcrumbs
- 1 large yellow sweet onion, sliced 1/2-inch thick and separated into rings
- 1/2 cup of buttermilk; see notes below for making your own
- 1 egg
- 1/2 cup of all-purpose flour
- Oil spray
- 2 tablespoons of olive oil
- 1 teaspoon of paprika
- 1 teaspoon of salt, divided

Instructions

1. You need four shallow bowls. Combine the paprika, flour, and 1/2 teaspoon of salt in the first bowl. Combine egg and buttermilk (or milk and vinegar/lemon juice) in the second bowl, then add 1/4 cup of the flour mixture from the first bowl. In the third bowl, add 1/2 teaspoon of salt, olive oil, and panko breadcrumbs and mix until the oil is evenly distributed. Place half of the panko mixture in a fourth bowl.

2. Pat the onion rings with a paper towel to remove any excess moisture. With a fork, lightly coat the onion rings with the flour mixture, and then dip them into the buttermilk mixture and then in the panko mixture. (Recipe tip: Freeze the breaded onion rings on a baking sheet for fifteen minutes to allow the panko mixture to stick better.)

3. Gently spray the Air Fryer basket with an oil spray. In the Air Fryer basket, arrange the onion rings in a single layer. If possible, you can set small rings inside larger rings, but make sure there is space between them.

4. Cook at 400°F for 11 to 15 minutes, or until they are crispy and golden brown. After about 6 minutes, spray with cooking spray.

5. With a cookie spatula or fork, gently lift out the onion rings and serve.

Notes

- For this recipe, make sure to use sweet onions. The breading does not work well with white and yellow onions.

- Coat the onion rings with a fork rather than your hands.

- Separate the panko breadcrumb mixture into two batches so you can turn to the second when the first becomes sticky.

- If you don't have buttermilk, make your own with 1/2 cup of milk and one tablespoon of vinegar or lemon/lime juice.

- If you don't have panko breadcrumbs, you can use normal breadcrumbs, but the result will be less crispy.

- Don't shake the basket; this will make the breading fall out. You don't need to turn the onion rings during the cooking process.

- Depending on your Air Fryer, you may need to preheat it.

- The amount of time it takes to cook varies depending on the type of Air Fryer you have. The onion rings take 12 to 15 minutes to cook, but some versions cook hotter or colder than others, so keep an eye on them.

Air Fryer Seasoned Asparagus

Prep Time: 2 minutes

Cook Time: 10 minutes

Servings: 4

Ingredients

- Olive oil cooking spray
- 1 bunch of asparagus
- Garlic salt

Instructions

1. Trim the stems off the asparagus about 2 inches.
2. Put the asparagus in the air fryer basket.
3. Lightly spray with olive oil and season with garlic salt.
4. Cook for 5 minutes at 390°F.
5. Check and turn the asparagus.
6. Cook for a further 5 minutes.
7. Serve.

Garlic-Herb Fried Patty Pan Squash

Prep Time: 15 minutes

Cook Time: 15 minutes

Servings: 4

Ingredients

- 1 tablespoon of olive oil
- 5 cups of halved small pattypan squash (about 1-1/4 pounds)
- 1/2 teaspoon of salt

- 1/4 teaspoon of dried thyme
- 1/4 teaspoon of pepper
- 2 garlic cloves, minced
- 1 tablespoon of minced fresh parsley
- 1/4 teaspoon of dried oregano

Instructions

1. Preheat the air fryer to 375° F. Put the squash in a large bowl. Add oil, garlic, oregano, thyme, pepper, salt over the squash; toss to coat evenly. Place the squash on a greased tray in the air fryer basket. Cook until tender, about 10 to 15 minutes, stir once in a while. Serve with parsley.

Air Fryer Potato Chips

Prep Time: 30 minutes

Cook Time: 15 minutes/batch

Servings: 4

Ingredients

- Olive oil cooking spray
- Minced fresh parsley, optional
- 2 large potatoes
- 1/2 teaspoon of sea salt

Instructions

1. Preheat the air fryer to 360° F. Cut the potatoes in very thin slices with a mandoline or vegetable peeler. Put them in a large bowl; add cold water in the bowl. Soak for 15 minutes; drain. Add more ice water and soak for an additional 15 minutes.
2. Drain the potatoes, put them on towels, and pat dry. Gently spray potatoes with cooking spray and season with salt. Place potato slices in a single layer on a

greased tray in the air-fryer basket. Cook for 15 to 17 minutes, stirring and turning every 5 to 7 minutes, until crisp and golden brown. Sprinkle with parsley, if desired.

Notes

Why do you soak potatoes in water before frying?

- Soaking potatoes before frying them removes the potatoes' natural starch, giving them a delightful crunch. It also prevents them from sticking to each other in the basket during the cooking process.

Why your chips are soggy?

- If your chips are soggy, place them back in the air fryer and cook for a little longer.

Air Fryer Vegetarian Momos

Prep Time: 25 minutes

Cook Time: 15 minutes

Servings: 4

Ingredients

- 1/4 cup of chopped green onions
- 3/4 cup of shredded cabbage
- 3/4 cup of chopped carrots
- 1 tablespoon of vegetable oil
- 16 wonton wrappers
- 1/4 cup of water, or as needed
- 1 teaspoon of soy sauce
- Cooking spray

Instructions

1. In a skillet, add vegetable oil over medium-high heat. Add carrots and cabbage to the skillet and cook for 3 to 4 minutes. Then add green onions and cook for a further 3 minutes.

2. Take the skillet off the heat and whisk the soy sauce into the cabbage mixture. Set aside for 10 minutes to cool down.

3. Preheat the air fryer to 325° F (165° C).

4. Put one tablespoon of cabbage mixture in the center of each wonton wrapper. Fold the wrapper around the filling to form the required Momo shape. If needed, use water to seal the edges.

5. Spray the momos with cooking spray and put them in the air fryer basket.

6. Cook momos for 5 minutes in the air fryer. Gently flip the momos and cook for 3 to 5 minutes more, or until they are crispy and golden brown.

Air Fryer Pumpkin Fries

Prep Time: 25 minutes

Cook Time: 15 minutes/batch.

Servings: 4

Ingredients

- 1 medium pie pumpkin
- 1/2 cup of plain Greek yogurt
- 1/8 teaspoon plus 1/2 teaspoon of salt, divided
- 2 tablespoons of maple syrup
- 2-3 teaspoons of minced chipotle peppers in adobo sauce
- 1/4 teaspoon of ground cumin
- 1/4 teaspoon of chili powder

- 1/4 teaspoon of pepper
- 1/4 teaspoon of garlic powder

Instructions

1. Mix the maple syrup, 1/8 teaspoon salt, chipotle peppers, and yogurt in a small bowl. Cover and refrigerate the sauce until serving.

2. Preheat the air fryer to 400° F. Peel the pumpkin and slice in half lengthwise, discard the seeds. Cut into 1/2-inch strips.

3. Put the pumpkin strips in a large bowl and toss with 1/2 teaspoon of salt, pepper, cumin, chili powder, and garlic powder.

4. Arrange the pumpkin on a greased tray in the air-fryer basket, don't overcrowd the pumpkin strips. Cook for 6 to 8 minutes, or until just tender. Toss the pumpkin to redistribute; cook for another 3 to 5 minutes, or until crispy and browned. Serve with sauce.

Zucchini Corn Fritters

Prep Time: 10 minutes

Cook Time: 12 minutes

Servings: 4

Ingredients

- 2 medium zucchinis
- 1 cup of corn kernels
- 1 medium potato, cooked
- 2 tablespoons of chickpea flour
- 2-3 garlic cloves, finely minced
- 1-2 teaspoon of olive oil
- Salt and pepper

For Serving:

- Ketchup or Yogurt tahini sauce

Instructions

1. Grate the zucchini with a grater. Mix grated zucchini with a little salt and leave it for 10 to 15 minutes. Then, using clean hands or cheesecloth, squeeze out any excess water from the zucchini.
2. Grate or mash the cooked potato.
3. In a bowl, combine the potato, chickpea flour, zucchini, corn, garlic, pepper, and salt.
4. Take two tablespoons of batter, shape it into a patty, and then put it on parchment paper.
5. Lightly brush oil onto each fritter's surface. Preheat the Air Fryer to 360° F.
6. Arrange the fritters on the preheated Air Fryer mesh in a single layer. Cook for 8 minutes.
7. Turn the fritters and cook for a further 3 to 4 minutes, or until well cooked and the desired color is obtained.
8. Serve with yogurt tahini sauce or ketchup.

Notes

- Cooking potatoes: cook the potatoes for 3 minutes in the microwave. Then, soak for a few minutes in cold water. Peel the potatoes, and grate or mash them.
- Add more flour if required. You can also use all-purpose flour instead of chickpea flour.
- For Yogurt tahini sauce - mix one teaspoon of tahini with 1/2 cup yogurt and season with salt according to taste.

Air-Fried Radishes

Prep Time: 10 minutes

Cook Time: 15 minutes

Servings: 6

Ingredients

- 3 tablespoons of olive oil
- 2-1/4 pounds of radishes, trimmed, cut, quartered (6 cups)
- 1 teaspoon of dried oregano, or 1 tablespoon of minced fresh oregano
- 1/8 teaspoon of pepper
- 1/4 teaspoon of salt

Instructions

1. Preheat the air fryer to 375° F. In a bowl, mix the radishes with the remaining ingredients. Place radishes on a greased tray in an air fryer basket. Cook for about 12 to 15 minutes or they are until crisp-tender, stirring occasionally.

Mexican Air Fryer Corn on the Cob

Prep Time: 3 minutes

Cook Time: 10 minutes

Servings: 3

Ingredients

- Low-calorie spray
- 3 corn on the cob, husks removed

For Toppings

- Chopped cilantro fresh coriander
- Salt

- Lemon Zest

Instructions

1. Preheat the air fryer to 400° F (200° C).
2. Place the corn on the cob in a bowl, spray with low-calorie spray, and season with salt.
3. Place the corn in the air fryer basket and cook for about 10 minutes, turning the corn a few times to ensure even cooking.
4. Take out from the air fryer once cooked and serve with a pinch of salt, lemon zest, and chopped cilantro on top.

Air Fryer Patatas Bravas

Prep Time: 30 minutes

Cook Time: 30 minutes

Servings: 6

Ingredients

For Potatoes:

- 8 cups (2 Litres) of cold water
- 4 (200g or 7 oz) medium new potatoes
- 1 bay leaf
- 1 teaspoon (about 2 g) of smoked paprika
- Salt to taste
- 1 teaspoon (about 2 g) of ground cumin
- Olive oil spray

For Sauce:

- 1 tablespoon (about 15 ml) of sherry vinegar
- 1/2 teaspoon (about 1 g) of hot paprika

- 1 (3 g) garlic clove
- 1/2 cup (60 g or 2 oz) of mayonnaise
- 1 tablespoon (about 15 g) of tomato sauce
- Salt and pepper, to taste
- 1/2 teaspoon (about 1 g) of dried mint

For Spice Blend:

- 1 teaspoon (about 2 g) of herbs de Provence
- 1 teaspoon (about 2 g) of adobo seasoning

Instructions

1. In a blender or food processor, blend all the sauce ingredients until smooth. Transfer into a bowl and cover with plastic wrap. Place in refrigerator until ready to use.
2. In a separate bowl, thoroughly combine the spices and set them aside.
3. Peel the potatoes and cut them into 1-inch cubes.
4. Boil the water in a saucepan, then add the potatoes, paprika, bay leaf, and cumin. Season with salt. Cover with a lid and cook for 10 minutes on high heat.
5. Take the pan from the heat and discard the water.
6. Place the potatoes in the air fryer basket. Set the air fryer temperature to 400° F (200°C) and cook for 15 minutes, or until golden brown.
7. Place in a bowl, sprinkle with spices and combine to coat.
8. Move to a serving dish and pour the prepared sauce over it.

Air-Fryer Green Tomato Stacks

Prep Time: 20 minutes

Cook Time: 15 minutes/batch

Servings: 8

Ingredients

- 2 medium green tomatoes
- Cooking spray
- 1/4 cup of mayonnaise
- 2 medium red tomatoes
- 8 slices bacon, warmed
- 1/2 teaspoon of pepper, divided
- 2 large egg whites, lightly beaten
- 1/4 teaspoon of grated lime zest
- 2 tablespoons of lime juice
- 1/4 teaspoon of dried thyme, or 1 teaspoon of minced fresh thyme
- 1/4 teaspoon of salt
- 1/4 cup of all-purpose flour
- 3/4 cup of cornmeal

Instructions

1. Preheat the air fryer to 375° F. Mix the thyme, lime zest and juice, mayonnaise, and 1/4 teaspoon of pepper in a bowl; refrigerate until serving.

2. Place flour in a shallow bowl. In a separate shallow bowl, place the egg whites. Combine salt, cornmeal, and 1/4 teaspoon of pepper in a third bowl.

3. Cut each tomato crosswise into four slices. Lightly coat each tomato slice in flour; shake off any excess. Gently dip into the egg whites, then in the cornmeal mixture.

4. Arrange tomatoes on a greased tray in the air-fryer basket; spritz with cooking spray. Cook for 4 to 6 minutes, or until golden brown. Flip; spritz with cooking spray. Cook for another 4 to 6 minutes, or until golden brown.

5. Stack one slice of green tomato, bacon, and red tomato for each serving. Serve with sauce.

Air Fryer Carrots

Prep Time: 10 minutes

Cook Time: 10 minutes

Servings: 4

Ingredients

- 1 tablespoon of avocado oil, or olive oil
- 1-pound of carrots, rinsed and peeled
- ⅛ teaspoon of black pepper, freshly cracked
- 1 tablespoon of balsamic vinegar
- ¼ teaspoon of salt, adjust to taste

Instructions

1. Peel the carrots and cut them into 2-inch-thick slices.

2. In a large bowl, mix the carrots with vinegar, oil, and seasoning. Toss the carrots thoroughly until they are uniformly coated.

3. Preheat the air fryer for 2 minutes at 375° F. In the fryer basket, spread the seasoned carrots in a single layer. Depending on the size of your air fryer, you may have to cook them in two batches.

4. Cook for about 10 to 12 minutes in an air fryer, shaking halfway through. Take out from the fryer and check the doneness. Shake the basket and air fry for 2 more minutes if you like it extra crispy.

Notes

- In your air fryer basket, make sure the carrots are spread out in a single layer.
- You can also use baby carrots in this recipe. Simply skip the cutting step and proceed with the remaining instructions.

Chapter 7: Air Fryer Snack Recipes

A balanced snack between meals can help you feel satisfied and avoid overeating at mealtime. Here is a collection of the best snacks that you can make in your air fryer for any occasion!

Apple Chips

Prep Time: 10 minutes

Cook Time: 20 minutes

Servings: 2

Ingredients

- One apple
- Pinch of salt
- ¼ teaspoon of ground cinnamon

Instructions

1. Preheat the air fryer to 350° F (180° C).
2. Using a mandolin or a sharp knife to thinly slice the apples.
3. Toss the apples with salt and cinnamon in a bowl.

4. Arrange half of the spiced apple slices in a single layer in the air fryer basket.

5. Cook for 8 to 10 minutes, turning and flattening them at least twice during the cooking process.

6. Gently take out the cooked apple chips and then repeat with the remaining apple slices.

Notes

- The easiest way to slice the apples is with a mandolin. If this isn't available, make sure to use a sharp knife.

- To ensure that the apple slices cook at the same time, make sure they are all the same thickness.

- If the slices aren't all the same size, split them into batches based on thickness and cook them together.

- Since an air fryer's temperature varies depending on the brand and model, keep an eye on the food.

- We recommend not cutting them too thin because they will burn instead of crisping up.

- Don't worry if your apple chips aren't fully crisp when they're cooked. They'll crisp up as they cool.

- Use pears instead of apples in this recipe for a different taste profile.

Air-Fried Mozzarella Sticks

Prep Time: 20 minutes

Cook Time: 15 minutes

Additional Time: 1 hour

Servings: 4

Ingredients

For Batter:

- 1/4 cup of all-purpose flour
- 1/2 teaspoon of salt
- 5 tablespoons of cornstarch
- 1/2 cup of water
- 1 tablespoon of cornmeal
- 1 teaspoon of garlic powder

For Coating:

- 5 ounces of mozzarella cheese, cut into 1/2-inch strips
- 1/4 teaspoon of dried oregano
- 1 tablespoon of all-purpose flour, or as needed
- 1 cup of panko breadcrumbs
- 1/4 teaspoon of dried basil
- 1/2 teaspoon of parsley flakes
- 1/4 teaspoon of onion powder
- 1/2 teaspoon of garlic powder
- 1/2 teaspoon of ground black pepper
- 1/2 teaspoon of salt

- Cooking spray

Instructions

1. In a large bowl, add the flour.
2. In a second wide, shallow bowl, whisk together the cornmeal, flour, water, garlic powder, salt, and cornstarch; mix into a batter the consistency of pancake batter. If required, adjust the ingredients to get the correct consistency.
3. In a third wide, shallow bowl, mix the onion powder, panko, parsley, salt, pepper, garlic powder, basil, and oregano.
4. Coat each mozzarella stick with flour. Dredge each stick in the batter and then roll in the panko mixture until completely coated. Repeat the process with the remaining sticks. Arrange the sticks in a single layer on a baking sheet. Freeze for at least 1 hour.
5. Set the air fryer to 400°F (200° C) according to the manufacturer's instructions. In the fryer basket, arrange a row of mozzarella sticks. Lightly coat with cooking spray. Cook sticks for about 6 minutes. Then open the air fryer and flip the sticks with tongs. Cook for another 7 to 9 minutes, or until golden brown.

Tater Tots

Prep Time: 2 minutes

Cook Time: 7 minutes

Servings: 4

Ingredients

- 16 ounces of frozen tater tots

Instructions

1. Preheat the air fryer to 400° F.
2. Place the frozen tater tots into the air fryer basket, just not more than halfway.
3. Cook the tater tots in the air fryer for about 7 to 9 minutes, shaking halfway through.

4. Take out the tots from the air fryer once done. Serve warm with a dipping sauce of your choice.

Chickpea Fritters with Sweet-Spicy Sauce

Prep Time: 20 minutes

Cook Time: 20 minutes

Servings: 4

Ingredients

- 1 tablespoon of honey
- 2 tablespoons of sugar
- 1/2 teaspoon of salt
- 1 cup of plain yogurt
- 1 can of chickpeas (15 ounces), rinsed and drained
- 1/2 teaspoon of salt
- 1/2 teaspoon of crushed red pepper flakes
- 1/2 teaspoon of garlic powder
- 1/2 teaspoon of ground ginger
- 1/2 cup of chopped fresh cilantro
- 1/2 teaspoon of pepper
- 1/2 teaspoon of baking soda
- 1 large egg
- 1 teaspoon of ground cumin
- 2 green onions, thinly sliced

Instructions

1. Preheat the air fryer to 400° F. Combine two tablespoons of sugar, one cup of plain yogurt, one tablespoon of honey, 1/2 teaspoon of pepper, and 1/2 teaspoon of crushed red pepper flakes in a bowl. Refrigerate until serving.

2. In a food processor, put the chickpeas and seasonings and process until finely ground. Add the baking soda and egg and pulse until blended. Put into a bowl; add green onions and cilantro, mix well.

3. Place rounded tablespoons of bean mixture into a greased tray in the air-fryer basket. Cook for about 5 to 6 minutes, or until lightly browned. Serve with sauce.

Air-Fryer Turkey Croquettes

Prep Time: 20 minutes

Cook Time: 10 minutes/batch

Servings: 6

Ingredients

- 3 cups of finely chopped cooked turkey
- 1 shallot, finely chopped
- 1/2 cup of shredded Swiss cheese
- 1/2 cup of grated Parmesan cheese
- 2 teaspoons of minced fresh rosemary, or 1/2 teaspoon of dried rosemary, crushed
- 2 cups of mashed potatoes (with added milk and butter)
- 1 teaspoon of minced fresh sage, or 1/4 teaspoon of dried sage leaves
- 1/2 teaspoon of salt
- 1-1/4 cups of panko breadcrumbs
- Butter-flavored cooking spray
- 2 tablespoons of water

- 1 large egg
- 1/4 teaspoon of pepper
- Sour cream, for serving

Instructions

1. Preheat the air fryer to 350° F. Combine the cheeses, mashed potatoes, shallot, sage, rosemary, salt, and pepper in a large bowl; then mix the chopped cooked turkey in it. Shape the patties into twelve 1-inch-thick patties.

2. In a shallow bowl, whisk together water and egg. Place breadcrumbs in a separate shallow bowl. Dip the croquettes in the egg mixture, then in the breadcrumbs, patting them down to ensure the coating sticks.

3. Arrange croquettes in a single layer on a greased tray in the air-fryer basket; spritz with cooking spray. Cook for about 4 to 5 minutes, or until golden brown. Flip; spritz with cooking spray. Cook for another 4 to 5 minutes, or until golden brown. Serve with sour cream, if desired.

Air Fryer French Fries

Prep Time: 10 minutes

Cook Time: 15 minutes

Servings: 2

Ingredients

- 1 medium russet potato (about 6 ounces), peeled
- Kosher salt and freshly ground black pepper
- 1 teaspoon of olive oil
- Non-stick cooking spray, for the basket

Instructions

1. Spray an air fryer basket with non-stick spray and preheat the air fryer to 380° F.

2. Slice the potato in half lengthwise, then cut into 1/4-inch slices. Make 1/4-inch sticks out of the slices. In a medium bowl, rinse the fries thoroughly with cold water, then drain and dry with paper towels.

3. In a medium bowl, toss the fries with the oil, then season with several grinds of pepper and 1/2 teaspoon of salt. Put the fries in an even layer in the air fryer basket with no overlapping and cook, until crispy and golden brown, for about 14 to 16 minutes, turning halfway through. Take out from the fryer once done and season with salt.

Air-Fryer Crispy Chickpeas

Prep Time: 10 minutes

Cook Time: 15 minutes

Servings: 3

Ingredients

- 2 tablespoons of red wine vinegar
- 1 (15-oz.) can of no-salt-added chickpeas (garbanzo beans), drained and rinsed (about 1 1/2 cups)
- 1/2 teaspoon of ground turmeric
- 1/4 teaspoon of ground coriander
- 2 tablespoons of olive oil
- 2 teaspoons of curry powder
- 1/4 teaspoon plus 1/8 teaspoon of ground cinnamon
- 1/4 teaspoon of ground cumin
- Thinly sliced fresh cilantro
- 1/2 teaspoon of Aleppo pepper
- 1/4 teaspoon of kosher salt

Instructions

1. In a medium bowl, gently smash chickpeas with your hands (do not crush), discard chickpea skins.

2. Add oil and vinegar to chickpeas and toss to coat. Add the coriander, cumin, curry powder, cinnamon, and turmeric; gently stir to combine.

3. Place chickpeas in an air fryer basket in a single layer and cook at 400°F for about 15 minutes, or until they get crispy, shaking the chickpeas halfway through cooking.

4. Transfer chickpeas to a bowl once done. Season with salt, cilantro, and Aleppo pepper; toss to coat.

Air fryer cheez-it recipe

Prep Time: 1 minute

Cook Time: 10 minutes

Servings: 2

Ingredients

- Cooking Spray
- 3 cups of Cheez-its
- Seasoning of choice (preferably Spank's BBQ)

Instructions

1. Put Cheez-its in a bowl.

2. Spray cooking spray on them. Gently shake the bowl a few times and spray again, ensuring all are coated with oil spray.

3. Cover generously with seasoning. Shake to coat the seasoning.

4. Cook for about 10 minutes at 240°F in the Air Fryer.

5. Serve.

Pepperoni Pizza Fries

Prep Time: 5 minutes

Cook Time: 25 minutes

Servings: 3

Ingredients

- 12 slices of pepperoni
- 1/2 cup of shredded mozzarella cheese
- 2 russet potatoes
- 1 tablespoon of olive oil
- 2 teaspoons of oregano
- Fresh parsley
- 1 teaspoon of sea salt
- 1/8 teaspoon of black pepper
- Tomato sauce, for dipping

Instructions

1. Wash and peel the potatoes, then cut them into quarter-inch matchstick fries.
2. Toss the fries with oregano, olive oil, black pepper, and salt in a large bowl.
3. Spread the fries uniformly in the air fryer basket, covering the entire bottom of the basket.
4. Preheat your air fryer to 400° F.
5. Set a timer for 20 minutes and toss every 5 minutes.
6. After 20 minutes, add the cheese and pepperoni slices.
7. Cook for 5 more minutes.
8. Gently remove the fries from the basket and put them on a serving plate.

9. Garnish with parsley.
10. If desired, serve with warm tomato sauce for dipping.

Air Fryer Apple Cinnamon Rolls

Prep Time: 10 minutes

Cook Time: 15 minutes

Servings: 8

Ingredients

- 1 ½ cups of self-raising flour (see note)
- 1 Apple (Cripps Pink), finely diced
- 2 tablespoons of unsalted butter, melted
- ½ cup of brown sugar
- 1 cup of Greek yoghurt
- 1 ½ tablespoons of cinnamon

Instructions

1. Preheat the air fryer to 180°C/350°F for 5 minutes.
2. In a mixing bowl, add Greek yogurt and stir well. Add 1 cup of flour and stir until it is well combined. Add more flour gradually until the dough begins to form a ball.
3. Place the dough on a floured surface and knead with your hands for a minute or two. If the dough is still sticky, add more flour and continue to knead. When the dough holds its shape and does not stick to your hands or the floor, it is ready.
4. Roll the dough into a rectangle shape with a well-floured rolling pin, then brush with butter and cover with brown sugar and cinnamon. Sprinkle apple pieces on top.
5. Roll the dough tightly and cut it into eight pieces. Arrange the pieces in your air fryer basket or tray, leaving enough space between them to cook properly. You will need to cook it in two batches if you have a smaller air fryer.

6. Cook for about 10 to 15 minutes, or until golden and cooked through. Once done, transfer to a wire rack to cool completely.

Notes

- Don't worry if you don't get a perfect rectangular shape. Simply roll it out as much as possible before topping it with butter, cinnamon, sugar, and apple.

- For Flour: If you don't have self-raising flour, combine the plain flour, all-purpose flour, and baking powder in a bowl. For each cup of all-purpose flour, you'll need two teaspoons of baking powder. So, if your dough uses 1 & ½ cups of flour, use three teaspoons of baking powder, and so on.

- These rolls can stick a little. Spraying a little cooking oil in the air fryer basket first will prevent them from sticking. Just make sure you're not using traditional spray oil from the supermarket because it can damage the non-stick coating. Brush your basket with oil if you don't have a mitzo, or something similar that sprays pure oil with no fillers.

- You'll have to work quickly with this dough because it gets stickier the longer it stays at room temperature, so roll it out, load it up, and roll it up as soon as you have the right consistency.

- After about 10 minutes in the air fryer, keep an eye on the rolls.

- For Storing: You can store the rolls once they have cooled completely, in an airtight container or Ziplock bag at room temperature for up to 2 days, or in the freezer for up to 3 months.

Air Fryer Roasted Almonds

Prep Time: 2 minutes

Cook Time: 8 minutes

Servings: 1 cup

Ingredients

- 1 cup of plain almonds

Instructions

1. Preheat the air fryer for 2 minutes at 350°F/180°C.
2. Place the almonds in the basket in a single layer and cook for 5 minutes. Give the basket a good shake and continue cooking until they're done, checking every minute.
3. Transfer to a bowl to cool properly. Once cooled, then store them in an airtight container or jar.

Notes

- Since almonds can quickly go from almost cooked to burnt, pay close attention to the cooking process (checking every minute after the first 5) is essential. When the almonds are a few shades darker and smell nutty, they're ready. Are you unsure if it's done? Take a bite—it should be crispy on the inside.
- Don't place them in an airtight jar or container before they've fully cooled. You can make more (or even less) almonds than one cup; just make sure they all fit in the basket in a single layer.

Air Fryer Falafels

Prep Time: 15 minutes

Cook Time: 15 minutes

Servings: 4

Ingredients

- 3 tablespoons of all-purpose flour (or all-purpose gluten-free flour, or chickpea flour)
- 1/2 cup of roughly chopped yellow onion (1 small yellow onion)
- 1 (15-oz.) can of chickpeas (garbanzo beans), drained
- 2 cloves of garlic, roughly chopped
- 1 teaspoon of ground cumin

- 1/4 teaspoon of coarse ground black pepper
- 3/4 teaspoon of kosher salt
- 1/2 cup of fresh cilantro, roughly chopped
- 1/2 cup of fresh parsley, roughly chopped
- 1/2 teaspoon of baking soda
- 1/8 teaspoon of cayenne powder
- 1/2 teaspoon of ground coriander

Instructions

1. Combine parsley, chickpeas, coriander, cayenne, baking soda, garlic, flour, onion, cumin, pepper, and salt in a food processor. Pulse until the mixture is coarse and mealy. Don't over-blend it.
2. Gently coat the bottom of the air fryer basket with olive oil spray. Shape the bean mixture into 1 1/2-inch diameter balls. Spray with olive oil spray and place in the air fryer basket with some space so they don't touch each other.
3. Air fry for about 12 to 14 minutes at 350° F, turning once, until golden.

Notes

- To use dry chickpeas, soak 3/4 cup dry beans in water for 24 hours. Add 1/2 teaspoon of baking soda to the soaking water. Rinse and drain soaked beans and proceed with the recipe as instructed.
- Make your falafel spicier by adding more garlic, cayenne, or red pepper flakes.

13. Air-Fryer Ravioli

Prep Time: 20 minutes

Cook Time: 10 minutes/batch

Servings: 5

Ingredients

- 1/4 cup of shredded Parmesan cheese
- 1/2 cup of all-purpose flour
- 1 package of frozen beef ravioli (about 9 ounces), thawed
- Fresh minced basil, optional
- 1 cup of seasoned breadcrumbs
- 2 teaspoons of dried basil
- 2 large eggs, lightly beaten
- For serving: 1 cup of marinara sauce, warmed
- Cooking spray

Instructions

1. Preheat the air fryer to 350° F. In a large bowl, mix the breadcrumbs, Parmesan cheese, and basil. In a second shallow bowl, add the flour. In a third shallow bowl, beat the eggs. Coat both sides of ravioli in flour; shake off the excess flour from ravioli. Dip in beaten eggs, then dredge in crumb mixture, gently pat to stick the coating.

2. Arrange ravioli on a greased tray in the air-fryer basket in single layer, spray with cooking spray; you may have to cook it in batches. Cook for about 3 to 4 minutes, or until golden brown. Turn, spray with cooking spray. Cook for a further 3 to 4 minutes, or until golden brown on all sides. If desired, sprinkle basil and additional Parmesan cheese. Serve warm with sauce.

Nutella Banana Sandwich

Prep Time: 10 minutes

Cook Time: 10 minutes

Servings: 2

Ingredients

- 4 slices of white bread
- Butter, softened
- 1 banana
- 1/4 cup of chocolate hazelnut spread Nutella

Instructions

1. Preheat the air fryer to 370° F.
2. Spread softened butter on one side of all the bread slices and put them on the plate, buttered side down. On the other side of the bread slices, spread the chocolate hazelnut spread. Cut the banana in half, then slice each half lengthwise into three slices. To make two sandwiches, layer the banana slices on two slices of bread and top with the remaining bread slices. Cut the sandwiches in half (triangles or rectangles) to fit in the air fryer at the same time. Place the sandwiches in the air fryer to cook.
3. Air-fry for 5 minutes at 370°F. Gently flip the sandwiches and air-fry for 2 to 3 minutes more, or until the bread slices are golden brown. Enjoy.

Mini Pizza

Prep Time: 10 minutes

Cook Time: 5 minutes

Servings: 16 mini pizza

Ingredients

- 1 can of Grands Biscuits
- 8 ounces of shredded mozzarella cheese
- 1 - 2 teaspoons of olive oil
- 1 cup of marinara sauce
- 1/2 pound of cooked sausage
- 4 ounces of pepperoni slices
- 2 tablespoons of all-purpose flour, for rolling

Instructions

1. Preheat the air fryer to 400° F for 5 minutes.
2. Separate the biscuits into two layers.
3. Lightly flour a cutting board and roll each biscuit half into a 3-inch circle with a rolling pin.
4. Spread two teaspoons of marinara sauce on top of each dough circle.
5. Add the pepperoni and sausage, and top with cheese.
6. Gently spray or brush olive oil into the air fryer basket.
7. Place pizzas in the air fryer basket with a spatula.
8. Cook at 400°F for 4 minutes, or until golden brown.
9. Place on a wire rack to cool and repeat with the remaining ingredients.
10. Serve pizzas right away, or let them cool fully on a wire rack before storing them in the refrigerator.

Notes

1. Cooled pizzas can be stored in zip-top bags in the refrigerator for up to 3 days.
2. Reheat in the air fryer for 2 minutes at 350°F.

Air Fryer Plate Nachos

Prep Time: 10 minutes

Cook Time: 5 minutes

Servings: 5

Ingredients

- Grilled chicken
- Green onions diced
- Tortilla chips
- Grape tomatoes, halved
- White queso
- Black beans, drained & rinsed

Instructions

1. Line the air fryer basket with foil. Spray with non-stick cooking spray.
2. Make the nachos by layering the chips, beans, and chicken in the air fryer basket.
3. Add a layer of white queso.
4. Add tomatoes and onions to the top.
5. Preheat the air fryer to 355°F and cook for 5 minutes.
6. Cook for additional time until your desired level of crispiness is achieved.

Beef Taco Fried Egg Rolls

Prep Time: 15 minutes

Cook Time: 25 minutes

Servings: 8

Ingredients

- 16 egg roll wrappers (preferably Wing Hing wraps)
- 1 pound of ground beef
- 2 garlic cloves, minced
- Cooking oil spray
- 1/2 cup of chopped red onion
- 1 cup of shredded Mexican cheese
- 16 oz can of dice tomato and chilies (preferably Mexican Rotel)
- 8 oz of refried black beans
- 1/2 cup of whole kernel corn

Homemade Taco Seasoning

- Salt and pepper, to taste
- 1 teaspoon of cumin
- 1 teaspoon of smoked paprika
- 1 tablespoon of chili powder

Instructions

1. In a skillet over medium-high heat, combine the ground beef, taco seasoning, salt, and pepper. Cook until the beef is browned.

2. Once the meat has started to brown, add the garlic and onion. Cook until the onions become fragrant.

3. Add the beans, diced tomatoes and chilies, Mexican cheese, and corn, in the beef skillet. Stir them together to ensure the mixture is combined.

4. On a flat surface, place the egg roll wrappers. Dip the cooking brush in water. Use the wet brush to glaze the edges of each egg roll wrapper. This softens the crust and makes it easier to roll.

5. Fill each wrapper with two tablespoons of the mixture. Don't stuff too much. You may need to double wrap the egg rolls depending on the brand of egg roll wrappers you use.

6. To close the wrappers, fold them diagonally. To keep the filling in place, press firmly on it and cup it. Fold in the right and left sides as triangles. Fold the final layer over the top to close. Use the cooking brush to wet the area and keep it in place.

7. Spray the cooking oil into the Air Fryer basket.

8. Place the egg rolls in the Air Fryer basket. Apply cooking spray on each egg roll.

9. Preheat the air fryer to 400°F and cook for 8 minutes. Flip the egg rolls. Cook for another 4 minutes, or until they are crispy and browned.

Notes

- You can use 1/2 packet of store-bought taco seasoning if you don't want to make the seasoning.
- Both sides must be golden brown. Depending on the type of Air Fryer used, the cooking time can vary.

Air Fryer Roasted Pineapple

Prep Time: 5 minutes

Cook Time: 15 minutes

Servings: 2

Ingredients

- 1 fresh pineapple

Instructions

1. Preheat the air fryer to 375° F (190° C).
2. Use parchment paper to line the air fryer basket.
3. With a pineapple corer or slicer, core the pineapple and slice it into rings. Place pineapple rings in the prepared basket.
4. Air fry for about 8 to 10 minutes, or until the slices start to roast. Turn the slices over and air fry for another 3 to 5 minutes.

Mac and Cheese Bites

Prep Time: 20 minutes

Cook Time: 6 minutes

Servings: 36

Ingredients

- 4 slices of bacon
- 1 egg
- 1 box of Macaroni & Cheese designed to serve 4 people (this is generally 1 larger deluxe 14-ounce box, or 2 small 7.5 ounce boxes)
- 1 cup of broccoli florets
- 1/2 cup of French fried onions
- 3/4 cup of cheddar cheese, shredded

Instructions

1. Prepare your mac and cheese according to the package directions.
2. While the mac and cheese is cooking, cook the bacon.
3. Add the broccoli to the mac and cheese in the last 2 to 3 minutes of cooking.
4. Once the mac and cheese is cooked, stir in the egg and crumbled bacon.
5. Spray the muffin cups with cooking spray. Then add about two tablespoons of mac and cheese mixture into each muffin cup. Gently push it down in the cups.
6. Top with a bit of cheddar cheese and fried onions into each muffin cup.
7. Place the muffin cups in the air fryer basket. Don't overload the air fryer basket because the air needs space to circulate.
8. Place the basket in the air fryer and cook for about 6 to 8 minutes at 400° F, or until they are golden brown on the edges. Use tongs to take the muffin cups out from the air fryer.
9. Set aside for 3 minutes to allow the mac and cheese bites to cool. Then pop them out of the muffin cups and set them on a serving plate.

Air Fryer Crab Cakes

Prep Time: 5 minutes

Cook Time: 10 minutes

Servings: 4

Ingredients

- 1 red bell pepper, de-seeded and chopped
- 1 teaspoon of lemon juice
- 8 ounces of lump crab meat
- 3 tablespoons of breadcrumbs

- 3 tablespoons of mayonnaise
- 3 green onions, chopped
- 2 teaspoons of Old Bay Seasoning
- Lemon wedges, for serving

Instructions

1. Preheat the air fryer to 370° F.
2. Add the green onions, breadcrumbs, lump crab meat, bell pepper, lemon juice, mayonnaise, and Old Bay Seasoning to a bowl, mix until well combined.
3. Gently shape four equal size crab patties.
4. Place a piece of parchment inside the hot air fryer, then carefully arrange the crab cakes in the air fryer.
5. In the air fryer, cook the fresh crab cakes for about 8 to 10 minutes, or until the crust is golden brown. Don't flip them while cooking.
6. Take the crab cakes out of the air fryer and serve with your favorite sauce and a squeeze of lemon on top, if desired.

Notes

How you can Reheat Crab Cakes in the Air Fryer?

1. Preheat the air fryer to 350° F.
2. Heat the leftover crab cakes in the air fryer for about 3 minutes, or until they are warm.
3. Take them out of the air fryer and serve!

How to Cook Frozen Crab Cakes in the Air Fryer?

1. Preheat the air fryer to 400° F.
2. Cook the frozen crab cakes in the air fryer for about 7 to 8 minutes, or until they are warmed fully.
3. Take them out of the air fryer and serve.

Crispy Air-Fried Buffalo Tofu

Prep Time: 15 minutes

Cook Time: 15 minutes

Servings: 4

Ingredients

- 1 small onion, cut into cubes
- 1 tablespoon of oil
- 1 package of Tofu, preferably extra firm (400 g)
- 4 stalks of spring onions/scallions with the greens, chopped
- 2 cloves of garlic, chopped finely
- 2 tablespoons of corn starch
- 1 small bell pepper, cut into cubes
- 2 tablespoons of brown sugar
- 1 teaspoon of chili sauce, adjust based on your tastes
- 2 tablespoons of Soy sauce
- ¼ teaspoon of salt
- 1 teaspoon of toasted sesame seeds, to garnish, optional
- ¼ teaspoon of crushed black pepper

Instructions

1. Drain the tofu well, wrap it in several paper towels and press it down with a weight to extract most of the liquid. Then, cut them into small cubes. Toss the chopped tofu with salt, corn flour, and pepper and mix properly.

2. Spray the tofu with a thin layer of oil and arrange it in a single layer in the preheated air fryer basket. Air fry for about 8 to 10 minutes at 400° F, or until golden brown. In between, toss the tofu a couple of times.

3. Heat one tablespoon of oil in a pan and add the bell pepper and onions.
4. Add garlic and spring onions and fry for a minute.
5. Add brown sugar, chili sauce, and soy sauce, and mix well.
6. To this, add the fried tofu and toss to combine the ingredients.
7. Transfer it to a serving dish and top with sesame seeds.

Notes

- To obtain a crisp texture, extract as much moisture from the tofu as possible.
- For the best results, use firm or extra-firm tofu.
- You can add more vegetables to make it a vegetable stir fry with tofu.
- Serve the Air Fryer tofu right after assembling, or else it could get soggy.

Air Fryer Corn Dogs

Prep Time: 0 minute

Cook Time: 8 minutes

Servings: 4

Ingredients

- 1 package of frozen corndogs

Instructions

1. In the air fryer basket, arrange the frozen corn dogs (no need to add oil). Air fry the dogs for about 6 to 8 minutes at 400°F/204°C.
2. Take out the basket from the air fryer. Plate your dogs and serve with your favorite dipping sauce; keep in mind that they are very hot.

Notes

- When putting the dogs in the air fryer basket, do not stack them. They need some space to cook.

- Should I thaw them? No, the hot dogs do not need to be thawed before cooking. You can cook them straight from the freezer!

- These hot dogs heat up quickly and stay hot for a long time. So be careful when removing them from the air fryer basket.

- What about the oil? There is no need to add any extra oil.

- Do the sticks burn in the air fryer? Some of the batter may burn where it meets the stick, but we haven't had any problems. You can break off the sticks if you don't feel satisfied.

Taco Lasagna

Prep Time: 15 minutes

Cook Time: 8 minutes

Servings: 6

Ingredients

- 4 flour tortillas, or corn tortillas or gluten-free tortillas
- 1 onion, chopped
- 2 cups (about 266g) of cheddar cheese, shredded
- 16 ounces (about 454g) of ground beef
- 1/2 cup (about 112g) of tomato sauce
- 1 teaspoon of oregano
- 2 tablespoons of olive oil
- 1/2 teaspoon of adobo
- 1 garlic clove, minced
- Salt and pepper, to taste
- 1 teaspoon of cumin

Instructions

1. In a pan, heat the olive oil and cook the onions until they soften.
2. Add ground beef and garlic and cook until the beef is browned.
3. Add tomato sauce and spices and bring to a simmer.
4. Start assembling the lasagna by putting a tortilla in the bottom of the air fryer basket.
5. Add a layer of beef, then a layer of cheese, and repeat the process. Finish with a final tortilla covered with cheese.
6. Cook for about 7 minutes in the air fryer at 350°F/176°C, or until the cheese is fully melted.

Notes

- If you want a spicier flavor, add chopped jalapeno when you cook the beef. You can also add spicy pepper jack cheese.
- Use plain canned tomato sauce, not spaghetti or pizza sauce, as those often have seasonings and Italian flavors added.
- Divide the beef mixture into three parts, so you finish with a tortilla layer. This will help the lasagna hold its shape and be evenly cut into single servings.

Fried Pork and Bok Choy Dumplings with Dipping Sauce

Prep Time: 30 minutes

Cook Time: 30 minutes

Servings: 6

Ingredients

- 1 tablespoon of garlic, chopped
- 4 ounces of ground pork
- 1/4 teaspoon of crushed red pepper

- Four cups of chopped bok choy (about 12 ounces)
- 1 tablespoon of fresh ginger, chopped
- 18 dumpling wrappers (3 1/2-inch-square)
- 1/2 teaspoon of packed light brown sugar
- 1 tablespoon of finely chopped scallions
- 1 teaspoon of canola oil
- 2 tablespoons of rice vinegar
- 2 teaspoons of soy sauce
- 1 teaspoon of toasted sesame oil
- Cooking spray

Instructions

1. In a large non-stick skillet, heat the canola oil over medium-high heat. Add bok choy and cook, stirring frequently, until wilted and mostly dry, for about 6 to 8 minutes. Add garlic and ginger and cook for one minute, stirring constantly. Put the bok choy mixture on a plate to cool for 5 minutes. Pat the mixture dry using a paper towel.

2. In a medium bowl, stir together the bok choy mixture, ground pork, and crushed red pepper.

3. Place a dumpling wrapper on the work surface and spoon one tablespoon of filling into the center. Lightly moisten the edges of the wrapper with water, using a pastry brush or your fingers. To make a half-moon shape, fold the wrapper over and press the edges together to seal. Fill the remaining wrappers with the filling and repeat the process.

4. With cooking spray, lightly coat the air fryer basket. Arrange the dumplings in the basket, leaving space between each; Gently spray the dumplings with cooking spray. Cook for about 12 minutes at 375°F, turning the dumplings halfway through. Repeat with the rest of the dumplings, keep the cooked dumplings warm.

5. To make the sauce: In a small bowl, whisk together soy sauce, brown sugar, sesame oil, rice vinegar, scallions, and mix until the sugar is fully dissolved. To serve, place three dumplings on each plate with two teaspoons of sauce.

Air-Fryer Caribbean Wontons

Prep Time: 30 minutes

Cook Time: 10 minutes/batch

Servings: 6

Ingredients

- 1 cup of marshmallow creme
- 24 wonton wrappers
- 1/4 cup of sweetened shredded coconut
- 2 tablespoons of walnuts, chopped
- 4 ounces of cream cheese, softened
- 1/4 cup of mashed ripe banana
- 2 tablespoons of canned crushed pineapple
- Cooking spray

For Sauce:

- 1/4 cup of sugar
- 1 teaspoon of cornstarch
- Ground cinnamon
- 1-pound of fresh strawberries, hulled
- Confectioners' sugar

Instructions

1. Preheat the air fryer to 350° F. In a bowl, beat the cream cheese until smooth. Stir in banana, pineapple, coconut, and walnuts. Then mix marshmallow creme in it.

2. Place a wonton wrapper with one point toward you. Cover the remaining wrappers with a damp paper towel until ready to use. Add two teaspoons of filling to the center of the wrapper. Wet the edges and fold opposite corners together over the filling, press to seal. Repeat with the remaining wrappers and filling.

3. Place the wontons in a single layer on a greased tray in the air-fryer basket, then spray with cooking spray. Cook for about 10 to 12 minutes, or until crispy and golden brown.

4. Put strawberries in a food processor and puree until smooth. Combine cornstarch and sugar in a small saucepan. Stir in blended strawberries. Bring to a boil, then cook and stir for 2 minutes, or until the sauce has thickened. Strain the mixture, store the sauce if desired; discard the seeds. Sprinkle wontons with cinnamon and confectioners' sugar. Serve with sauce.

Chapter 8: Air Fryer Dessert Recipes

Delicious treats are filled with extra calories and carbohydrates, but with an air fryer, you can make nutritious treats that you can enjoy guilt-free! You can make your desserts more nutritious by changing the recipes, adding balanced ingredients, and, of course, with an air fryer. Here are some delicious dessert recipes that you will absolutely love.

Grilled Peaches

Prep Time: 5 minutes

Cook Time: 10 minutes

Servings: 2

Ingredients

- 1/4 cup of graham cracker crumbs
- 2 yellow peaches
- 1/4 cup of butter, diced into tiny cubes
- Whipped Cream or Ice Cream
- 1/4 cup of brown sugar

Instructions

4. Remove the pits from the peaches and cut them into wedges.
5. Place a piece of parchment paper on top of the rack in the Air Fryer.
6. Place the peach wedges on parchment paper, skin side up (on the side).
7. Air fry for 5 minutes at 350°F.
8. Combine the butter, crumbs, and brown sugar in a bowl.
9. Turn the peaches' skin side down.
10. Spoon the crumb mixture on top of peaches; try to keep the butter on top of the peaches as much as possible.
11. Air fry for a further 5 minutes at 350°F.
12. Spoon peaches onto plates with a large spoon.
13. Top with whipped cream.
14. Spoon any remaining butter/topping mixture left on the parchment onto whipped topping.

Air Fryer S'mores

Prep Time: 5 minutes

Cook Time: 5 minutes

Servings: 4

Ingredients

- 4 marshmallows
- 8 squares of Hershey's chocolate bar, broken into individual squares
- 4 graham crackers (each broken in half to make 2 squares, for a total of 8 squares)

Instructions

1. Arrange four graham cracker squares in the Air Fryer basket.

2. On each cracker, place two chocolate bar squares.

3. Place the basket in the air fryer and cook for 1 minute at 390° F, or until the chocolate melts. This should be just enough time for the chocolate to melt. Take the air fryer basket out of the fryer.

4. Place a marshmallow on top of each cracker. Press the marshmallow a little to the melted chocolate. This will help to stick the marshmallow to the chocolate.

5. Return the basket to the air fryer and cook for 2 minutes at 390°F. (The marshmallows should be puffy and starting to brown on top.)

6. Carefully remove each cracker from the Air Fryer basket with tongs and place it on a plate. Place a second graham cracker square on top of each marshmallow!

7. Serve.

Air Fryer Oreos

Prep Time: 5 minutes

Cook Time: 10 minutes

Servings: 10

Ingredients

- 8 Oreo cookies
- 1-2 tablespoons of powdered sugar
- 1 can of Crescents Dough

Instructions

1. Cover the Oreo cookies with the crescent dough; make sure there are no air bubbles, and the Oreo is fully coated.

2. Arrange the covered Oreos on the Air Fryer rack and cook for about 4 minutes at 350° F.

3. Turn the Oreos once the tops are a light golden brown, about 3 to 4 minutes.

4. Once the Oreos are done, dust them with powdered sugar before serving.

Air Fryer Apple Crisp

Prep Time: 10 minutes

Cook Time: 25 minutes

Servings: 2

Ingredients

- 2 chopped apples
- 2 tablespoons of brown sugar
- 1 teaspoon of lemon juice
- 1 teaspoon of cinnamon

For Topping:

- 3 tablespoons of old-fashioned oats
- 2 tablespoons of brown sugar
- 1 pinch of salt
- 2 ½ tablespoons of flour
- 2 tablespoons of cold butter

Instructions

1. Preheat the air fryer to 350°F. With butter, grease a 5-inch oval baking dish.
2. Peel the apples, core them, and cut them into small cubes. Combine the apples, sugar, cinnamon, and lemon juice in a bowl. Pour the mixture into the baking dish.
3. Cover the dish with aluminum foil and bake for 15 minutes. Open the air fryer and continue cooking for 5 more minutes uncovered.
4. In the bowl of an electric mixer fitted with the paddle attachment, combine cold butter, sugars, flour, salt, and oatmeal, to make the topping. Mix on low speed until the butter is the size of peas and the mixture is crumbly. Spread evenly over the apples.

5. Move the crisp apple mixture to the air fryer, uncovered, and cook for 5 minutes.
6. Serve with melted caramel sauce, whipped topping, or vanilla ice cream on top.

Air Fryer Brownies

Prep Time: 10 minutes

Cook Time: 20 minutes

Servings: 6

Ingredients

- 1 Egg
- ¼ cup of cocoa powder
- 4 tablespoons of salted butter
- ¼ cup of all-purpose/plain flour
- ¼ cup of white sugar
- ¼ cup of brown sugar
- ½ teaspoon of vanilla
- ⅕ cup of chocolate chips

Optional

- ¼ cup of chunks of your favorite chocolate

Instructions

1. Line 2 mini loaf pans or 1 regular loaf pan with baking paper.
2. In a microwave-safe bowl, add brown sugar, cocoa powder, butter, and white sugar. Microwave in 20-second batches, mixing well after each time, until the butter is melted and well combined.
3. Whisk in the vanilla and mix thoroughly. Set aside the bowl for a minute to cool slightly.

4. Mix in the egg, then add flour and properly mix until well combined. Fold in the chocolate chips and add the chocolate chunks if using.

5. Evenly distribute the mixture among the prepared mini loaf pans (or only pour into one loaf pan if that's what you're using), and bake for 20 to 25 minutes in the Air Fryer, or until a toothpick inserted into the center comes out with just a few fudgy particles attached.

6. Allow 10 minutes for the brownies to cool in the loaf pans, then move to a wire rack to cool completely.

Notes

- The chocolate chunks are not necessary, but they are highly recommended. Cut your favorite chocolate bar into tiny chunks and add it to the brownie mixture.

- You can use two mini loaf pans or one regular loaf pan. As long as it fits in your Air Fryer, it will work.

Strawberry Cheesecake Chimichangas

Prep Time: 20 minutes

Cook Time: 20 minutes

Servings: 6 chimichanga

Ingredients

- 6 (8-inch) soft flour tortillas
- 1 package of cream cheese (at room temperature)
- 1/4 cup of sour cream
- 1 tablespoon of cinnamon
- 1 tablespoon of sugar
- 1/4 cup of sugar
- 1 3/4 cups of sliced strawberries

- 1 teaspoon of vanilla extract
- 1/2 teaspoon of fresh lemon zest

Instructions

1. Beat the cream cheese with sour cream, lemon zest, one tablespoon of sugar, and vanilla extract in the bowl of a stand mixer fitted with the paddle attachment; scraping down the sides of the bowl as needed.
2. Gently fold in 3/4 cup of sliced strawberries.
3. Microwave the tortillas for about 30 to 45 seconds; it will allow them to bend easier.
4. Uniformly distribute the mixture among the tortillas, slathering each part in the lower third of each tortilla.
5. Fold the two sides of each tortilla toward the middle and roll it up like a burrito, securing it with a toothpick.
6. Roll the remaining tortillas in the same way.
7. In a shallow bowl, combine 1/4 cup of sugar and the cinnamon. Set aside.
8. Preheat your Air Fryer to 400° F.
9. In the Air Fryer basket, arrange the chimichangas.
10. Spray the chimichangas with cooking spray.
11. Set the time for 6 minutes.
12. Take the chimichangas from the basket after 6 minutes.
13. Roll them in a mixture of cinnamon and sugar.
14. Put the chimichangas on serving plates after removing all toothpicks.
15. Garnish each chimichanga with strawberry slices and serve right away.

Air Fryer Beignets

Prep Time: 10 minutes

Cook Time: 15 minutes

Additional Time: 15 minutes

Servings: 4

Ingredients

- 1/2 cup of powdered sugar
- 1 cup of plain Greek yogurt
- 1 cup of self-raising flour
- 1 tablespoon of vanilla
- 2 tablespoons of melted unsalted butter
- 2 tablespoons of sugar

Instructions

1. In a bowl, combine sugar, yogurt, and vanilla.
2. Stir in the flour until the mixture starts to form a dough.
3. Place the dough on a floured surface.
4. Fold the dough in half a couple of times.
5. Make a 1-inch-thick rectangle out of the dough. Then cut it into 9 pieces. Gently dust each piece with flour.
6. Set aside for 15 minutes.
7. Preheat the Air Fryer to 350° F.
8. Spray the Air Fryer basket or tray with canola oil spray.
9. Using melted butter, brush the tops of your dough.
10. Place in a basket or tray with the butter side down. Brush the dough's tops with butter.

11. Cook for about 6 to 7 minutes, or until the sides of the beignets begin to brown.
12. Flip over and cook for further 6 to 7 minutes.
13. Dust with powdered sugar.

Monkey Bread

Prep Time: 5 minutes

Cook Time: 20 minutes

Servings: 6

Ingredients

- ¼ cup of sugar
- 1 can of biscuit dough
- 6 tablespoons of melted butter
- ½ cup of brown sugar
- 1 teaspoon of cinnamon

Instructions

1. Cut each biscuit dough into quarters. Take each piece and roll it into a ball. Put the dough balls in a bowl and set them aside.
2. Mix brown sugar and melted butter. Set aside.
3. Combine cinnamon and white sugar in a bowl. Pour it over the dough and mix well.
4. Coat the inside of the Air Fryer pot or oven-safe dish with spray oil. Put the dough mixture into the pot.
5. Pour the brown sugar and melted butter mixture evenly over the dough.
6. Air fry for 18 to 20 minutes at 320° F or 160° C. Once done, take out from the Air Fryer and set aside for 5 minutes to cool. Gently turn the monkey bread upside down onto a plate and enjoy!

Apple Fritters with Brown Butter Glaze

Prep Time: 10 minutes

Cook Time: 10 minutes

Servings: 5

Ingredients

For Brown Butter Glaze

- 1/4 cup of butter (1/2 stick)
- 1/2 teaspoon of vanilla
- 1 tablespoon of milk, if needed
- 1 cup of powdered sugar

For Apple Fritters

- 2 large Apples (like Honey Crisp or Green Apples), peeled, cored, and diced in small pieces
- Vegetable or canola oil, for brushing/spraying
- 1 1/2 cups of all-purpose flour
- 1 tablespoon of lemon juice, fresh
- 2 eggs
- 1/4 cup of granulated sugar
- 2 teaspoons of baking powder
- 1/3 cup of milk
- 1/2 teaspoon of salt
- 1 1/2 teaspoon of ground cinnamon
- 1 teaspoon of vanilla

Instructions

For Brown Butter Glaze

1. In a small saucepan, melt the butter over medium-high heat. Melt the butter until it fizzes and turns brown. Remove from heat once browned and set aside to cool slightly. The butter should have a nutty scent and brown specks.

2. In a small bowl, add the powdered sugar. Mix the milk, browned butter, and vanilla until smooth. (If the mixture is too thin, add more powdered sugar.) Set aside.

For Apple Fritters

1. Line the basket of the Air Fryer with a piece of parchment paper. You can cut parchment paper to the required size so that the edges won't overlap. Brush a thin layer of oil on the surface or use an oil spray.

2. In a medium bowl, mix sugar, flour, salt, cinnamon, and baking powder.

3. Make a well in the center and add the vanilla, eggs, lemon juice, and milk, and mix it properly. Fold the apples in the mixture.

4. Depending on the Air Fryer's size, set the fritters into the air fryer basket. If you overcrowd the air fryer at one time, then the fritters won't get crispy.

5. Use a pastry brush or an oil sprayer to lightly coat the top of the fritters with oil. Set the air fryer to 400° F and cook the fritters for 4 to 5 minutes until they are golden brown. Flip fritters and cook until both sides are golden brown.

6. Arrange apple fritters on the rack and drizzle with butter glaze while fritters are still warm.

Notes

- If the glaze is too thin, just add more powdered sugar or reduce the amount of milk.

Air Fryer Lava Cake

Prep Time: 15 minutes

Cook Time: 10 minutes

Servings: 2

Ingredients

- 2 eggs
- 4 tablespoons of butter
- 3 tablespoons of all-purpose flour
- 1/2 cup of semi-sweet chocolate chips
- 1 teaspoon of vanilla extract
- 1/2 cup of powdered sugar
- 1/4 teaspoon of salt

For the Nutella Filling

- 1 tablespoon of butter, softened
- 1 tablespoon of powdered sugar
- 2 tablespoons of Nutella

Instructions

1. Preheat the air fryer to 370° F.
2. Melt the chocolate chips and butter in a medium microwave-safe bowl in 30-second intervals, stirring at each interval, until fully melted and smooth.
3. Whisk together the flour, eggs, powdered sugar, vanilla, and salt in the melted chocolate chip bowl.
4. Combine Nutella, powdered sugar, and softened butter in a separate bowl.

5. Spray the ramekins with cooking spray and fill them halfway with the chocolate chip mixture. Add the Nutella filling in the center of the ramekin, then layer the chocolate chip mixture, making sure the Nutella is completely covered.

6. Gently put the lava cakes in the Air Fryer and cook for about 8 to 11 minutes.

7. Carefully take out the lava cakes from the Air Fryer and set them aside to cool for 5 minutes. Take a butter knife, run it around the outside edges of the cake, and flip out onto a serving dish.

8. Serve with chocolate syrup, ice cream, or other toppings.

Air Fried Banana

Prep Time: 10 minutes

Cook Time: 10 minutes

Servings: 2

Ingredients

- 1/4 teaspoon of cinnamon
- 1 ripe banana, cut into ½-inch slices
- 1/2 teaspoon of brown sugar
- 1 tablespoon of chopped toasted nuts, to taste
- 1 tablespoon of granola, to taste

Instructions

1. Mix brown sugar and cinnamon in a small bowl and set aside.

2. Lightly grease a shallow baking pan with cooking spray. In the pan, place the banana slices. Spray the banana slices with oil and then sprinkle with cinnamon sugar. Air fry for about 4 to 5 minutes at 400°F (200°C).

3. To serve, sprinkle some nuts and granola over the banana.

Air Fryer Blueberry Pie Egg Rolls

Prep Time: 20 minutes

Cook Time: 25 minutes

Servings: 4

Ingredients

- 2 cups of blueberries
- Olive oil or butter-flavored cooking spray
- 12 egg roll wrappers
- 1 teaspoon of lemon zest
- ½ cup of agave nectar
- 1 tablespoon of cornstarch
- 1 tablespoon of lemon juice
- Confectioner's sugar, for dusting
- 2 tablespoons of water

Instructions

1. In a saucepan, combine water, blueberries, lemon zest, agave nectar, and cornstarch.
2. Stir thoroughly to dissolve the cornstarch in the water.
3. Over medium-high heat, bring it to a boil. Reduce the heat and simmer for about 5 minutes, or until the berries begin to break down and the sauce has thickened, stirring occasionally.
4. Take it from the heat and add the lemon juice. Set aside to cool.
5. Now, take an egg roll wrapper and place it diagonally in front.
6. Fill the lower end of the wrapper with about two tablespoons of the filling.

7. Roll up the wrapper halfway, then fold in the right and the left sides, like an envelope. Then roll to the very end, sealing the roll with a little water.

8. Repeat with the remaining wrappers.

9. Arrange a few prepared rolls in the Air Fryer basket and lightly spray with either olive oil or butter-flavored cooking spray.

10. Air fry for 5 minutes at 370°F.

11. Continue with the rest of the rolls. While the rolls are still hot, lightly dust them with confectioner's sugar.

12. Serve right away.

Air Fryer Twix Cheesecake

Prep Time: 15 minutes

Cook Time: 1 hour 5 minutes

Servings: 10

Ingredients

For Cookie Crust

- 1 cup of powdered sugar
- 1 ½ sticks of butter, melted
- 1 ½ cups of flour

For Cheesecake

- 1 teaspoon of lemon juice
- 2 eggs
- 32 oz of cream cheese, softened
- 1 ½ cup of powdered sugar
- ½ package of jello instant cheesecake pudding 3 oz size
- ¼ cup of heavy cream

For Topping

- 3 squares of chocolate almond bark melting chocolate
- ⅓ cup of heavy cream
- 1 jar of caramel ice cream topping

Instructions

For Crust

1. In a bowl, whisk together powdered sugar and flour. Melt butter in the microwave and mix into the powdered sugar/flour mixture. Properly stir the butter into the mix.
2. Place Parchment paper in the bottom of a 7-inch Spring-form pan. Pour the flour mixture into the pan and press it firmly into the bottom.
3. Place the pan in the Air Fryer for 6 minutes at 350° F.

For Cheesecake

1. Put softened cream cheese in the mixing bowl of a stand mixer, and blend until smooth.
2. Add eggs, and lemon juice, and mix until the eggs are well blended. Add the instant pudding to the heavy cream and mix until smooth.
3. Pour the pudding into the mixing bowl. Add powdered sugar and mix on low until smooth.
4. Scrape down the sides of the bowl and blend until it is fully blended. Take out the pan from the Air Fryer and pour the cheesecake mixture into the Springform pan. Bake in the Air Fryer at 350° F for 55 minutes.
5. After 10 minutes, take out the cheesecake from the Air Fryer and cover it loosely with foil. Return it to the Air Fryer to finish cooking.
6. When the cheesecake is done, remove it from the Air Fryer and set it aside for 30 minutes (with the Air Fryer switched off). Place it on a wire rack to cool.

7. Once the cheesecake has cooled, wrap it in foil and put it in the refrigerator to set overnight. Take out the cheesecake from the refrigerator the next day, spoon the caramel topping on top, and put it back in the fridge.

For Topping

1. Place the heavy cream in a microwave-safe dish and microwave until hot. Don't boil. Put three squares of chocolate in the hot cream and mix to melt the chocolate. If the chocolate doesn't fully melt, return it to the microwave for another 15 seconds and mix until it's smooth and melted.

2. Place the cheesecake on a serving plate.

3. Pour the melted chocolate over the cheesecake and allow it to run down the sides and onto the serving plate. Put the cheesecake back in the refrigerator until ready to serve to allow the chocolate to set. Enjoy! Serve on dessert plates.

Notes

- You can replace the Jello pudding in the cheesecake with a different flavor.
- When making cheesecakes, a springform pan is ideal.
- Take the cheesecake's internal temperature. It should reach a temperature of 145°F. This way, you can be sure your cheesecake is completely baked.
- Make your cheesecake at least one day in advance, as the cheesecake will need to set overnight in the fridge. Then, take it out and top with your caramel and chocolate.

Air Fryer Banana Muffins

Prep Time: 5 minutes

Cook Time: 15 minutes

Servings: 5

Ingredients

- ⅓ cup of olive oil
- 1 egg
- 2 very ripe bananas
- 1 teaspoon of cinnamon
- ½ cup of brown sugar
- ¾ cup of self-raising flour (see notes)
- 1 teaspoon of vanilla extract

Instructions

1. Preheat the Air Fryer to 160°C / 320°F for 5 minutes.
2. In a large bowl, mash the bananas, then add brown sugar, egg, vanilla extract, and olive oil. Stir well to combine.
3. Divide the mixture evenly into muffin cases (paper or silicone) and gently place them into the Air Fryer basket.
4. Bake for 15 minutes, or until golden and a skewer inserted into the center comes out clean. You may need to do it in two batches if you have a smaller air fryer.
5. Transfer the muffins to a wire rack to cool.

Notes

- The Air Fryer browns the muffins faster than the oven, but this does not affect the taste.

- If you live in America, don't use self-raising flour as the recipe instructs. Store-bought American self-raising flour includes salt (as it's usually used for biscuits). Instead, use 1.5 teaspoons of baking powder and 3/4 cup of all-purpose flour.
- Only use very ripe bananas; otherwise, you won't get that delicious banana flavor.
- For this recipe, use silicone muffin cases or double-up paper cases.

Air Fryer Jelly Donuts

Prep Time: 10 minutes

Cook Time: 5 minutes

Servings: 8

Ingredients

- 1/2 cup of seedless raspberry jelly
- 1 tablespoon of butter, melted.
- One package of Pillsbury Grands (Homestyle)
- 1/2 cup of sugar

Instructions

1. Preheat the air fryer to 320° F.
2. Arrange Grand Rolls in a single layer in the Air Fryer and cook for 5 to 6 minutes, or until golden brown.
3. Remove the rolls from the Air Fryer and place them on a plate to cool.
4. Place the sugar into a wide bowl.
5. Brush the donut with butter on all sides and roll it in sugar to fully cover it. Repeat with the remaining donut.
6. Pipe 1 to 2 tablespoons of raspberry jelly into each donut with a long cake tip.
7. Serve right away.

Conclusion

As an overall useful appliance, the Air Fryer makes an excellent contribution to your kitchen. Air fryers can cook many more recipes than a deep fryer and can even be used for grilling steaks or baking pizzas.

It's like getting a deep fryer and an oven in one device, and it fits on your kitchen countertop, not occupying much space. Some versions can also be used as a pressure cooker, and a dehydrator, and can cook a whole rotisserie chicken. Yes, it's an all-in-one appliance. The fryer can replace many other appliances in your kitchen because it can cook a wide variety of delicious meals, not just those usually cooked by frying.

In the summer, using a fryer will not heat your home. You can see how using a fryer makes cooking faster, and how it is more efficient than using traditional appliances.

Air fryers eliminate high-fat and high-calorie oils from the cooking process. Instead of fully submerging the food in oil, air-frying only takes a tablespoon to achieve the same flavor and texture as deep-fried foods. Although Air Fryers are a better alternative to deep fryers, the best option for your health is to reduce your intake of high fats.

Make sure you thoroughly analyze your needs before buying an Air Fryer, regardless of the type of Air Fryer you choose. The ideal Air Fryer will last for years and gives you plenty of delicious meals.

www.ingramcontent.com/pod-product-compliance
Lightning Source LLC
Chambersburg PA
CBHW081349080526
44588CB00016B/2425